国际中文教育武术技术推广系列教材
Wushu Techniques Textbook Series for International Chinese Edu

国际武术联合会
International Wushu Federation
中国武术协会
Chinese Wushu Association
北京体育大学汉语国际推广武术师资培训基地
Wushu Teacher Training Base for Chinese International Promotion of Beijing Sport University

南　拳
Nan Quan

高楚兰　主编
袁　哲　译

北京体育大学出版社

策划编辑：佟　晖
责任编辑：潘海英
责任校对：赵红霞
版式设计：李　鹤

图书在版编目（CIP）数据

南拳 : 汉英对照 / 高楚兰主编 ; 袁哲译. -- 北京:
北京体育大学出版社, 2022.6（2022.11重印）
ISBN 978-7-5644-3660-5

Ⅰ.①南… Ⅱ.①高… ②袁… Ⅲ.①南拳 – 基本知
识 – 汉、英 Ⅳ.①G852.13

中国版本图书馆CIP数据核字(2022)第093118号

南拳
NANQUAN

高楚兰　主编
袁　哲　译

出版发行：北京体育大学出版社
地　　址：北京市海淀区农大南路1号院2号楼2层办公B-212
邮　　编：100084
网　　址：http://cbs.bsu.edu.cn
发 行 部：010-62989320
邮 购 部：北京体育大学出版社读者服务部 010-62989432
印　　刷：北京建宏印刷有限公司
开　　本：710 mm×1000 mm　　1/16
成品尺寸：170 mm×240 mm
印　　张：17.75
字　　数：314千字
版　　次：2022年6月第1版
印　　次：2022年11月第2次印刷
定　　价：100.00元

国际中文教育武术技术推广系列教材

组织机构

教育部中外语言交流合作中心

北京体育大学

国际武术联合会

中国武术协会

审定委员会

吴　彬　门惠丰　金肖冰

编写委员会

总　主　编：李士英

副总主编：高楚兰　佟　晖

分册主编：王二平　李士英　李英奎

　　　　　林小美　高楚兰

国际中文教育武术技术推广系列教材
《南拳》编委会

主　编：高楚兰

副主编：王继娜

编　委：郑磊石　　段永斌　　陶凌荣

示　范：刘博雅

译　者：袁　哲

目录 Contents

1

武礼篇

Wushu Etiquette

　　中华武术历史悠久，源远流长，内容丰富多彩、博大精深。源于中国，属于世界的武术运动，深受世界各国人民喜爱，已成为全人类共有的精神、文化财富。

Chinese Wushu (martial arts) goes back to time immemorial, and is well-established, long-standing, and profound. Originating from China, Wushu also belongs to the world, and is greatly admired by people all over the world; it has become a spiritual and cultural asset shared by all.

一、武 礼　　Wushu Etiquette

　　"未曾习武先习礼"，武礼是中国传统的礼法之一。武礼现已成为在国际上一致采用的、具有代表性的、规范统一的武术标准礼法。

　　武礼的行礼方式包括徒手礼（抱拳礼、注目礼）、持械礼、递械礼和接械礼等。

"Before practicing Wushu, acquire relevant etiquette first." Wushu etiquette is part of China's traditional cultural rule of etiquette, and has become a common practice in the international Wushu community.

Wushu etiquette is represented by barehanded salutes (palm-fist salute; eye salute), weapon-holding salute, weapon-delivering salute, and weapon-receiving salute.

1. 抱拳礼 Palm-fist salute

抱拳礼的行礼方式是：并步站立，左手四指并拢伸直成掌，拇指屈拢，右手成拳，左掌心掩贴右拳面，左指根线与右拳棱相齐；左掌、右拳胸前相抱，高度与胸平齐，肘尖略下垂，拳、掌与胸间距为20~30厘米；头正，身直，目视受礼者。（图1-1）

抱拳礼的含义是：左掌为文，象征和平，代表武德，寓意孝敬父母、尊敬师长、爱国敬业、诚信友善、仁爱感恩、谦卑简朴；拇指弯曲表示谦虚，寓意武术源于中国，属于世界，应虚心好学、永不自大。右拳为武，象征力量，代表武技，寓意尚武崇德、追求卓越、为国争光、为民服务。左掌盖在右拳上表示爱心、礼让、止戈为武。两手相合，表示习武者要文武兼备、内外兼修，五湖四海天下武林是一家，以武会友、友好团结，弘扬武学文化，造福人类。抱拳礼的寓意为和平、团结和友谊。

The palm-fist salute is as follows: stand with your feet together; the four fingers of your left hand stay straight together as an open palm, with the thumb bent and close to the index finger; the right hand forms a fist, with knuckles pressed against the center of the left palm, and the left palm's finger base line aligned with the right fist's metacarpophalangeal joint line. The fist and palm stay together 20-30 cm away from in front of your chest, with the tips of both elbows slightly drooping. Keep your head and body upright, and gaze at the one receiving the salute. (Fig. 1-1)

The palm-fist salute means: the left palm stands for erudition, symbolizing peace and martial ethics, and implying filial piety to parents, respect for teachers, patriotism, dedication, honesty and friendliness, benevolence and gratitude, humility, and frugality; the bent thumb means modesty, implying that Wushu originates from China and belongs to the world, and that those practicing Wushu should be humble and studious, but never arrogant. The right fist stands for martial arts, symbolizing strength and skills, implying the pursuit of virtue and excellence, glory for the country, and service to the people. The left palm is covered on the right fist to express love, comity, and truce.

The fist meets the palm to indicate that those practicing Wushu must be a master of both the pen and sword, in other words, to be well versed in both polite letters and martial arts. The world's Wushu community is a big family; Wushu is practiced to meet with friends, maintain friendship and unity, and to promote Wushu culture to benefit humanity. In short, the palm-fist salute symbolizes peace, unity, and friendship.

图 1-1　抱拳礼
Fig. 1-1 Palm-fist salute

2. 注目礼 Eye salute

　　注目礼的行礼方法是：并步站立，目视受礼者或向前平视，身体正直，以示对受礼者的恭敬、尊重。若表示答诺或聆听指教受益时，可微点头示意。

　　The eye salute is as follows: stand with your feet together; gaze at the recipient or look straight ahead; keep your body upright to show respect for the recipient. To respond to an eye salute, you can nod your head slightly.

3. 持械礼   Salute with a weapon

持械礼是习练武术器械时行的礼节，礼仪内涵同"抱拳礼"。

（1）持剑礼的行礼方法是：并步站立，左手持剑，屈臂，使剑身贴前臂外侧，斜横于胸前；右手拇指屈拢，成斜侧立掌（或剑指），以掌外沿附于左手食指根节，高度与胸平齐，肘微下垂，目视受礼者。（图1-2）

Saluting with a weapon is an etiquette to follow when practicing a weapon, and means the same as the palm-fist salute.

(1) Salute with a sword: stand with your feet together, hold the sword in your left hand, bend your arms, and the blade is attached to the outer edge of the left forearm and diagonally across the chest. Your right palm (or sword finger) stays oblique with the thumb bent, and the palm's outer edge is attached to the joint of the left hand's index finger. This position is at the height where the chest is, with the elbows slightly drooping and eyes on the recipient. (Fig. 1-2)

图 1-2　持剑礼
Fig. 1-2 Sword-holding salute

（2）抱刀礼的行礼方法是：并步站立，左手抱刀，屈臂，使刀横于胸前，刀身斜向下，刀背贴附于前臂之上，刀刃向上；右手拇指屈拢成斜侧立掌，以掌心附在左手拇指第一指节上，高度与胸平齐，肘微下垂，目视受礼者。（图1-3）

(2) Salute with a broadsword: stand with your feet together, hold the broadsword with your left hand, and bend your arms so that the broadsword is horizontal to the chest; the blade is slanted downward, with its spine attached to your forearm, and its belly facing upward. Your right palm stays oblique with the thumb bent, and the palm is attached to the first knuckle of the left thumb. This position is at the height where the chest is, with the elbows slightly drooping and eyes on the recipient. (Fig. 1-3)

图 1-3 抱刀礼
Fig. 1-3 Broadsword-holding salute

（3）持枪礼的行礼方法是：并步站立，右手握枪端，屈臂于胸前，枪身直立，枪尖向上；左手拇指屈拢成侧立掌，掌心与右手指根节指面相贴，高度与胸平齐，肘略下垂，目视受礼者。

(3) Salute with a spear: stand with your feet together, hold the spear in your right hand, with the arms bent in front of the chest; keep the spear upright, with its tip facing upward; keep your left palm in an oblique position with the thumb bent; the palm is in

contact with the right hand's finger joints. This position is at the height where the chest is, with the elbows slightly drooping and eyes on the recipient.

（4）持棍礼的行礼方法是：并步站立，右手握棍把段（靠棍把1/3处），屈臂于胸前，棍身直立，棍梢向上；左手拇指屈拢成侧立掌，掌心与右手指根节指面相贴，高度与胸平齐，肘略下垂，目视受礼者。（图1-4）

(4) Salute with a stick: stand with your feet together, hold the handle of the stick with your right hand (1/3 of the handle), with your arms bent in front of the chest; keep the stick upright, with its tip facing upward; keep your left palm in an oblique position with the thumb bent; the palm is in contact with the right hand's finger joints. This position is at the height where the chest is, with the elbows slightly drooping and eyes on the recipient. (Fig. 1-4)

图 1-4　持棍礼
Fig. 1-4 Stick-holding salute

4. 递械礼　　　　　　　　　　　　　Weapon-delivering salute

递械礼包括递剑礼、递刀礼、递枪礼和递棍礼等。

（1）递剑礼的行礼方法是：并步站立，左手托护手盘，右手托剑前身，使剑平横于胸前，剑尖向右，目视接剑者。

（2）递刀礼的行礼方法是：并步站立，左手托护手盘，右手托刀前身，使刀平横于胸前，刀刃向里，目视接刀者。

（3）递枪礼的行礼方法是：并步站立，双手靠近握枪于把段处，左手在上，两臂屈圆，使枪垂直于体前，枪尖向上，目视接枪者。

（4）递棍礼的行礼方法是：并步站立，双手靠近握棍于把段（靠棍把1/3处），左手在上，两臂屈圆，使棍垂直竖于体前，棍梢向上，目视接棍者。

其他器械的递械礼参照上述规范统一。

The weapon-delivering salute includes the sword-delivering salute, broadsword-delivering salute, spear-delivering salute, and stick-delivering salute etc.

(1) The sword-delivering salute is as follows: stand with your feet together, hold the cross-guard in your left hand, and support the front section of the blade with your right hand, so that the sword stays horizontal across the chest, with the tip of the sword pointing to the right and eyes on the recipient.

(2) The broadsword-delivering salute is as follows: stand with your feet together, hold the cross-guard in your left hand, and support the front section of the broadsword with your right hand, so that the broadsword stays horizontal across the chest, with the belly of the broadsword facing inward, and eyes on the recipient.

(3) The spear-delivering salute is as follows: stand with your feet together, hold the spear with both hands close to the handle, with your left hand on top and arms rounded; the spear stays vertical in front of your body, with the spear tip facing upward and your eyes on the recipient.

(4) The stick-delivering salute is as follows: stand with your feet together, keep your

hands close and hold the stick by the handle (1/3 of the stick), with your left hand on top and arms rounded, so that the stick stays vertical in front of your body, with the tip of the stick facing upward and your eyes on the recipient.

For the delivering of other weapons, please refer to the above-mentioned methods.

5. 接械礼　　　　　　　　　　　　　　　Weapon-receiving salute

接械礼包括接剑礼、接刀礼、接枪礼和接棍礼等。

（1）接剑礼的行礼方法是：开步站立，左手掌心向上，托剑于递剑者两手之间，右手手心向下接握剑柄，目视右手，接剑。

（2）接刀礼的行礼方法是：开步站立，左手掌心向上，托刀于递刀者两手之间，右手手心向下接握刀柄，目视右手，接刀。

（3）接枪礼的行礼方法是：开步站立，两手虎口向上，上下靠拢，左手在上，靠近递枪者手上部接握，目视双手，接枪。

（4）接棍礼的行礼方法是：开步站立，两手虎口向上，上下靠拢，左手在上，靠近递棍者手上部接握，目视双手，接棍。

其他器械的接械礼参照上述规范统一。

The weapon-receiving salute includes the sword-receiving salute, broadsword-receiving salute, spear-receiving salute, and stick-receiving salute etc.

(1) The sword-receiving salute is as follows: stand with your feet apart; your left palm faces upward and supports the sword between the deliverer's hands, and your right palm faces downward and holds the hilt of the sword; eyes on the right hand when receiving the sword.

(2) The broadsword receiving salute is as follows: stand with your feet apart; your left palm faces upward and supports the broadsword between the deliverer's hands, and your right palm faces downward and holds the hilt of the broadsword; eyes on the right hand when receiving the broadsword.

(3) The spear-receiving salute is as follows: stand with your feet apart; the part of the hand between the thumb and the index finger faces upward; hands stay close, with your left hand above your right hand and the deliverer's hands; eyes on both hands when receiving the spear.

(4) The stick-receiving salute is as follows: stand with your feet apart; the part of the hand between the thumb and the index finger faces upward; hands stay close, with your left hand above your right hand and the deliverer's hands; eyes on both hands when receiving the stick.

For the receiving of other weapons, please refer to the above-mentioned methods.

二、武礼的应用 　　　　　　Applying Wushu Etiquette

1. 技术教学训练课 　　　　　Technical training sessions

　　队长整队完毕，向老师报告时，师生均行"注目礼"。老师向学生说"上课！"，队长发"敬礼！"口令，学生行"抱拳礼"；老师看学生都行礼端正后，行"抱拳礼"答谢，落手立正；然后学生再落手立正。礼毕，授课开始。

　　授课结束，队长整队完毕，老师对本节课的整体情况进行总结发言后示意队长发"敬礼！"口令，学生行"抱拳礼"；老师看学生都行礼端正后，行"抱拳礼"答谢，落手立正；然后学生再落手立正。礼毕，老师向学生说"下课！"，老师和学生同时击掌，下课。

After the team leader lines everyone up and reports to the instructor, both the instructor and students salute with their eyes. The instructor says to the students, "Class!", then the team leader gives the "Salute" instruction, and the students perform the palm-fist salute. The instructor will make sure that all students are saluting properly and respond to them with the same position. The instructor then puts down his hands and resumes the position of attention; the students will do the same. After this, the session begins.

At the end of the session, the team leader again lines everyone up, and the instructor recaps on the session and then signals the team leader to give the "Salute" instruction. Then the students perform the palm-fist salute, and the instructor will make sure that all students are saluting properly and respond to them with the same position. The instructor then puts down his hands and resumes the position of attention; the students will do the same. After this, the instructor says, "Class dismissed", and gives students a high five before they leave the class.

2. 专业理论课 Theoretical sessions

老师走上讲台，向学生说"上课！"，队长发"起立！敬礼！"口令，学生行"抱拳礼"；老师看学生都行礼端正后，行"抱拳礼"答谢，落手立正；然后学生再落手立正，队长发"坐下！"口令。礼毕，学生就座，授课开始。

授课结束，老师向学生说"下课！"，队长发"起立！敬礼！"口令，学生行"抱拳礼"；老师看学生都行礼端正后，行"抱拳礼"答谢，落手立正；然后学生再落手立正，队长发"坐下！"口令。礼毕，学生就座，下课。

The instructor walks up to the podium and says to the students, "Class!", and the team leader follows by shouting out "Stand up! Salute!" The students then perform the palm-fist salute. The instructor will make sure that all students are saluting properly and respond to them with the same position. The instructor then puts down his hands and resumes the position of attention; the students will do the same. The team leader then shouts out "Sit down"! After this, the students are seated, and the session begins.

At the end of the session, the instructor says, "Class dismissed". The team leader shouts out "Stand up! Salute!", then the students perform the palm-fist salute. The instructor will make sure that all students are saluting properly and respond to them with the same position. The instructor then puts down his hands and resumes the position of attention; the students will do the same. The team leader then shouts out "Sit down"! After this, the students are seated, and the session ends.

3. 武术比赛、表演等　　　　　Wushu competition and performance

在武术测试、比赛时，运动员听到点名后应立即进场，面向裁判长，行"抱拳礼"或"持械礼"，待裁判长示意后，即走向起势位置；完成套路后，须并步收势，再转向裁判长行"抱拳礼"或"持械礼"，即可退场；赛后示分时应向裁判长行"抱拳礼"或"持械礼"。

在武术表演时，表演开始前和结束后，表演者应向主席台上的贵宾、前辈和观众行"抱拳礼"或"持械礼"。在武术的社会活动中，表演者受到介绍时应行"抱拳礼"示礼。在交流技术、切磋技艺时，双方也应行"抱拳礼"或"持械礼"。武林同道见面问候、告别时，也应行"抱拳礼"，以体现尊师重道，礼尚往来。

During tests or competitions, athletes should enter the arena immediately upon hearing their names called out, face the referee, and perform the palm-fist salute or weapon-holding salute; after the referee gestures, athletes should go to the starting position, complete the routine, stand at the finishing position, and then turn to the referee to perform the palm-fist salute or weapon-holding salute before leaving the arena. When the scores are announced, athletes should perform the palm-fist salute or weapon-holding salute to the referee.

When performing Wushu, before and after the performance, performers should do the palm-fist salute or weapon-holding salute to the distinguished guests on the rostrum, seniors, and spectators. On social occasions of Wushu, when being introduced, performers should perform the palm-fist salute to show etiquette. When exchanging techniques and discussing skills, both sides should perform the palm-fist salute or weapon-holding salute. When Wushu colleagues greet each other or say goodbye, they should also perform the palm-fist salute to show respect for the instructor and courtesy.

南拳概述

Overview of Nan Quan

一、认识南拳   Get to Know Nan Quan

南拳为流传于中国长江以南各地诸多拳种的统称。其流传的地域主要包括广东、广西、福建、湖南、湖北、四川、江西、江苏、浙江等。南拳在四百多年前已被载入史册，在历史的发展中，南拳形成了各具特色的不同流派。

广东南拳以洪家拳、刘家拳、蔡家拳、李家拳、莫家拳五大流派为主，还有蔡李佛拳、虎鹤双形拳、佛家拳、侠家拳、刀家教、岳家教、朱家教等。福建南拳主要流传有五祖拳、连城拳、白鹤拳、五祖白鹤拳，还有五形拳、猴拳、少林拳、梅花拳、罗汉拳等流派。四川南拳也有着悠久的历史，现在的派系主要有僧门拳、岳门拳、赵门拳、杜门拳、洪门拳、化门拳、字门拳、会门拳八大流派。湖南南拳有巫、洪、薛、岳四大流派。湖北南拳分为洪、鱼、孔、风、水、火、字、熊八门。江西南拳有字、硬两门。浙江南拳有洪家、黑虎、金刚三大拳系。另外，还有温州南拳、台州南拳和苏州南拳等。

Nan Quan refers to a variety of Chinese martial arts originated from the south of the Yangtze River of China, including Guangdong, Guangxi, Fujian, Hunan, Hubei, Sichuan, Jiangxi, Jiangsu, Zhejiang, etc. With a history of more than 400 years, its development has helped it form different schools with their own characteristics.

The styles of Nan Quan popular in Guangdong Province are primarily Cantonese family styles of Hong (Hung), Liu (Lao), Cai (Choi), Li (Lee), and Mo (Mok), together with more variants of Cai Li Fo (Choi Lee Fut), Tiger & Crane Fists, Fojia (Buddhist Fist), Xiajia, Diaojia, Yuejia, and Zhujia etc. Fujian Nan Quan mainly include styles like Wuzuquan (Five Ancestors Fist), Lianchengquan, Baihequan (White Crane) and Wuzu & Baihe, as well as Wuxingquan (also called the Five Elements Fist, imitating the forms of dragon, tiger, leopard, snake and crane), Houquan (Monkey Fist), Shaolinquan, Meihuaquan, and Luohanquan. Sichuan Nan Quan also has a long history. The eight contemporary styles are Sengmenquan, Yuemenquan, Zhaomenquan, Dumenquan, Hongmenquan, Huamenquan, Zimenquan and Huimenquan. For Hunan Nan Quan, Wu, Hong, Xue and Yue are the four main family styles. In Hubei province, Nan Quan is divided into Hong, Fish, Kong, Wind, Water, Fire, Zi and Bear. Zi and Ying are the two styles in Jiangxi; Hongjia, Heihu, and Jingang are in Zhejiang. In addition to those mentioned above, there are Wenzhou Nan Quan, Taizhou Nan Quan and Suzhou Nan Quan.

二、南拳特点　　　　　Characteristics of Nan Quan

1. 稳马硬桥　　　　　Steady "horse", hard "bridge"

南拳中的"马"即为"桩步"，是步型、步法的统称。所谓"稳马"，就是要求桩步沉实、稳固。南拳的步型要求高而不浮，低而不板，进退闪转灵活。马步和弓步是南拳中的主要桩步，站桩时要求五趾抓地，落地生根，经常练习站桩就是为了提高腿部的沉实和稳固，腿部沉实了，步势才能稳扎。"桥"是南拳中特有的一种手法。桥法即是臂的运行方法。"硬桥"的意思是只有把手臂练得像铜锤一样坚硬，才能在攻防的对抗中得心应手，与他人交手接触时，自己不至于受伤。南拳的桥法，大都用于防守，如截桥、架桥、缠桥、圈桥、穿桥、滚桥等。

The "horse" stance in Nan Quan is "Zhuangbu", which is a general term for step form and step position. "Steady horse" means that the "Zhuangbu" is solid and stable. For Nan Quan, the step form is required to be high but not floating, low but not rigid, and flexible in advancing and retreating. Horse stance and bow stance ("Gongbu") are the main stance steps in Nan Quan. When practicing Zhanzhuang (standing as a technique for developing internal energy), five toes are required to grasp the ground and take root on it. to practice this stance is to improve the solidity and stability of the legs. "Qiao (Bridge)", a unique technique in Nan Quan, is the movements of the arm. "Hard bridge" means that only by practicing the arm as hard as a copper hammer can you be adept in the confrontation of offense and defense, and will not be injured when coming into contact with others. The bridge techniques of Nan Quan are mostly used for defense, such as Jieqiao (cutting bridges), Jiaqiao (building bridges), Chanqiao (wrapping bridges), Quanqiao (encircling bridges), Chuanqiao (crossing bridges), Gunqiao (rolling bridges), etc.

2. 刚劲有力　　　　　　　　　　　　　　　Firm and powerful

　　南拳的发劲尽管分有短劲、长劲、弹抖劲、爆发劲等，但一般说来，刚劲有力是南拳的共同特点。如何做到刚劲有力呢？其一要注意发力的顺序，"力从腰马生"，腿、腰、背、肩及全身的协调一致，使力贯穿顺达，这是掌握南拳发劲的关键。正如拳家所说："力，其根在脚，发于腿，宰于腰，形于手。"如完成一个弓步冲拳，要先由半马步过渡，并且配合闭气蓄劲，然后通过蹬脚、扣膝、合胯、转腰、冲拳的由下而上的顺序发力；再如一个马步冲拳，要先闭气蓄劲，然后转腰顺肩冲拳，不能只注重梢节（拳）的"拉劲"，而没有注意根节（腿和腰）的"催劲"。其二要蓄发充分。南拳的发劲，强调在发劲前要有一个闭气蓄劲的过程，通过闭气，做到内紧（意识）外松（肌肉）；通过呼气发力，达到以气催力，加大动作始发的速度和爆发性用劲。如若发的是长劲，则应该打深、打透，不能为了求快而发一半劲。其三要力点准确、明显。南拳的技术动作大都讲究攻防含义，凡是进攻性动作，在演练时都要表现出明显的发力点，如南拳竞赛套路第四段的拖步冲拳接插步鞭拳接翻身挂盖拳，其中的冲拳、鞭拳和挂盖拳必须有明显的发力点，否则就体现不出南拳刚劲有力的风格特点。

　　Although Nan Quan's exertion of strength ("jin") is divided into short strength, long strength, bouncing strength, explosive strength, etc., generally speaking, to be firm and powerful are the common characteristics of Nan Quan. How to be firm and powerful? First, pay attention to the order of strength exertion. "Strength is born from the waist and the 'horse' (legs)"—then comes the coordination of the legs, waist, back, shoulders and the whole body, so that the strength can run smoothly, which is the key to mastering the strength of Nan Quan. As Wushu masters say: "Strength is rooted in the feet, developed by the legs, directed by the waist, and expressed in the hands." To complete "Thrust fist in a bow stance", you must first transit from a half horse stance, holding your breath to accumulate energy, and then exert strength in a bottom-up direction by kicking with heel, twisting the knee and hip, turning the waist, and punching; as another example, for "Thrust fist in a horse stance", you must first hold your breath and store up energy, then turn your waist and follow your shoulders to punch, you can't just focus on the tips (fist) "pulling" without paying attention to the "pushing" of the roots (legs and waist). Second, fully accumulate energy before releasing it. In the process of energy exertion, it is emphasized that there must be a phase of closing the breath and accumulating energy before releasing it. By holding your breath, the inside (consciousness) is tightened, and the outside (muscles) loosened. By exhaling, the force can be achieved by using the qi to increase initial speed and explosive force. If you are using long strength, you should exert deeply and thoroughly instead of using half of your energy for the sake of speed. Third, the point of exertion must be accurate and obvious. Most of Nan Quan's technical movements are about how to attack and defend. In all attacking movements, the point of exertion must be obvious, e.g., Tuobu Chongquan (Thrust fist in a dragging step), Chabu Bianquan (Whip fist in a back cross-step), Fanshen Guagaiquan (Fists swing overhead with the body turning around) in the fourth section of the Nan Quan Taolu (Routine) competition. There must be obvious point of exertion in Chongquan (Thrust fist), Bianquan (Whip fist) and Guagaiquan (Fists swing overhead), otherwise they will not reflect the firm and powerful characteristics of Nan Quan.

3. 手法丰富   Rich hand techniques

南拳的上肢手法较其他拳种丰富，不仅有拳法、掌法、勾法，而且有爪法、指法、肘法和桥法，其中桥法更是区别于其他拳种的显著特点之一。南拳练习通常在步型不变的情况下连续完成若干次上肢动作，故有"一势多手，一步几变手"的说法。南拳多短拳，擅标手，跳跃、腿法动作少。其腿法也大多采用踢、钉、踹、踩、弹等屈伸性腿法和少部分扫转性腿法，起腿一般要求高不过腰。跳跃动作多以跃步、跨步和中国武术教程其他小跃步为主。故武术谚语中有"南拳北腿"之说。

The hand techniques of Nan Quan are richer than that of other quan styles, including not only techniques of fist, palm, hook hand, but also of claw, finger, elbow and bridge, among which the bridge is one of the distinguishing features that make it different from other styles. In Nan Quan practice, one usually completes several upper body movements in a row without changing the step form. Therefore, there is a saying that goes "for one posture, there are rich hand techniques; for one step, there are changes of hand techniques". There are more short punches in Nan Quan. Practitioners are good at Biaoshou (exerting force to dissolve the attack from above), and has fewer jumping and leg movements, most of which use leg positions of kicking with lower leg such as kicking, nailing, kicking with sole, stepping, and bouncing, and a small number of which use sweeping-rotating leg position, where legs are generally required to be lower than the waist. Most of the jumping movements are leaps, strides and other small jumps. Hence comes a saying in martial arts "Leg of North and Fist of South".

4. 脱肩团胛   Shoulder sinking and scapula protraction

南拳的身法讲究脱肩团胛。脱肩，是指两肩有意识地向下沉坠；团胛，是使肩胛骨向前微合，形成团状。脱肩下沉，有助于臂、肘的合力；团胛前合，使背部收紧，有助于发劲前的蓄劲。

For the body position of Nan Quan, practitioners are required to sink their shoulders and mover forward their shoulder blades (scapula). Shoulder sinking refers to consciously moving the two shoulders downwards; scapula protraction means slightly making the shoulder blades move forward to form a lump. Shoulder sinking is helpful for the combined force of the arms and elbows; moving the shoulder blades forward tightens the back and helps to store up energy before releasing it.

5. 直项圆胸   Straight neck and "round" chest

南拳的身法还讲究直项圆胸。直项就是要求下颌里收，颈部伸直；圆胸，就是要求胸微内含，稍呈圆形。直项有助于胸、背、肩、肘的劲力合一；圆胸则有助于沉气实腹，闭气蓄劲。

The movement of Nan Quan also requires practitioners to have straight neck and round chest. Straight neck requires mandibular retraction, i.e., drawing back or retracting the chin to make the neck straight; "round" chest means drawing in the chest, i.e., chest slightly moving backward to make it slightly rounded. A straight neck helps create a unified strength of the chest, back, shoulders, and elbows; a "round" chest helps the qi to sink and keep stomach solid so that the qi is held to accumulate strength.

6. 气沉丹田   Bring qi down to dantian

南拳非常讲究气沉丹田，强调沉气实腹，使腹肌也参与收缩。沉气实腹，促使臀部必须收敛。它与脱肩团胛、直项圆胸及脚趾抓地乃是一个整体，做到上下完整一体，周身劲力就会凝结到一处，形成整力。

Bringing qi down to dantian is a key point in practicing Nan Quan. It emphasizes that qi is sank and absorbed in the stomach, and the abdominal muscles are also involved in the contraction. Concentrate on your stomach, so that your hips must be restrained. This movement is integrated with the shoulder sinking and scapula protraction, the straight neck and the round chest, and the toes gripping the ground. When the upper and lower parts are completely integrated, the strength of the whole body will be condensed in one place to form a cohesive force.

7. 节奏铿锵　　　　　　　　　　　　　　　　　　　Forceful rhythm

　　在武术的套路演练中，不论是哪个项目，都讲究演练的节奏。所谓节奏，实际上就是如何处理快慢、顿挫的问题。不同的拳种，有不同的节奏。"铿锵"，即为明快干脆，衡朗有声。南拳的动作虽然有快、有慢，但快必须是方法清楚，动作到位，发力明显，绝不是拖泥带水地快；即便是慢，动作也是刚劲有力，如单、双推指手，要求肌肉极限收缩而隆起，直项圆胸，脱肩团胛，沉气实腹，以气催力，均匀而缓慢地用劲向前推出，在身体的外形上表现出一种"体刚劲粗"的特点。

Practicing Wushu Taolu, whatever the competition event, involves the rhythm of the practice. Rhythm, in effect, means the way to deal with speed (rapid or slow), pause and transition. Rhythms are different in various quan styles. "To be forceful" means to be clear, swift and powerful in the movements which can be fast or slow. To be fast, the movement must be done smoothly. It must meet the requirements in a clear way and with obvious strength exertion. Even if one practices a slow movement, it has to be strong and powerful. For example, in single-finger-pushing and double-finger-pushing exercises, it has to meet the following requirements: muscles have to be contracted to the limit, the neck is straight, the chest is round, the shoulders sink, the shoulder blades move forward, qi is brought down and absorbed in the stomach. Afterwards, achieve the force by using the qi, and then push it evenly and slowly so that a physical characteristic of "strong body and powerful strength" is formed.

8. 拳势刚烈   Forceful quanshi

拳势，即气势。其他拳种称之为"精、气、神"。南拳的"呼喝则风云变色，开拳则山岳崩秃"特点，是区别于其他拳种的又一个特点，如稳健沉实的步法、饱满刚烈的发劲、抑扬顿挫的节奏，以及体格建壮、肌肉发达的形体等都是表现这一特点的重要因素。南拳在套路演练时，还讲究发声呼喝，通过合理的发声，一是助拳势，二是助发力，三是助形象，四是有利于排除体内余气；此外，在意识的运用和面部的表情上，也要注意合理而巧妙地配合。南拳在演练时，一般要意识内守、含蓄，面部表情略带怒意，眉宇微内收，全神贯注于每一招、每一势，做到意、气、形要整，有种拳势威猛、气势逼人的演练效果。

Quanshi refers to the momentum or, the imposing style of quan. It is called "Inner essence, Qi, and Spirit" in other quan styles. Nan Quan distinguishes itself from other quan styles when "one's shout is powerful enough to make a drastic change of the weather, and one's punch is fierce enough to make the mountains collapse". Steady and solid footwork, full and vigorous power, speed, pause and smooth transition, as well as a strong and muscular body are all important factors to embody this characteristic. Nan Quan also stresses the way to utter a shout when practicing routines. A good uttering can help strengthen quanshi and the exertion of strength, improve the image, and also remove the residual qi in the body. In addition, you should also pay attention to the good coordination of the use of consciousness and facial expressions. When practicing Nan Quan, you should keep the inner essence and qi with a slightly angry facial expression and slightly retracted eyebrows, and focus on every move, so that your yi (mind), qi, and xing (form) are integrated to create a powerful and forceful effect.

南拳基本动作

Basic Movements of Nan Quan

一、手　型　　　　　　　　　　　　　　　　　　　　Hand Forms

1.平拳　　　　　　　　　　　　　　　　　　　　　　　　Level fist

五指卷屈握紧，拳面要平，拇指压于食指和中指的第二指节上，任何指骨都不得凸出拳面。（图3-1）

Curl the five fingers and clench them tightly with the fist face flat. Press the thumb on the second knuckle of the index finger and middle finger, and no finger joint should extend beyond the fist face. (Fig. 3-1)

图 3-1　平拳
Fig. 3-1 Level fist

2.掌　　　　　　　　　　　　　　　　　　　　　　　　　　Palm

拇指弯曲，其余四指伸直并拢。（图3-2）

Bend the thumb and keep the remaining four fingers straight and together. (Fig. 3-2)

图 3-2　掌
Fig. 3-2 Palm

3. 虎爪 Tiger claw

五指用力张开，第二、三节指骨弯曲，第一节指骨尽量向手背的一面伸张，使掌心凸出。（图3-3）

Stretch out the five fingers, bend the second and third knuckles with the first one stretched to the back of the hand as far as possible, so that the palm is protruding. (Fig. 3-3)

图 3-3　虎爪
Fig. 3-3 Tiger claw

4. 鹰爪 Eagle claw

拇指弯曲外展，其余四指并紧，使第二、三节指骨弯曲，但不得屈拢。（图3-4）

Bend the five fingers by stretching the thumb outward and putting the other four fingers together. Bend the second and third knuckles but do not bend them over. (Fig. 3-4)

图 3-4　鹰爪
Fig. 3-4 Eagle claw

5.鹤嘴手   Crane's beak

五指捏拢，直腕。（图3-5）

Pinch the five fingers together; keep the wrist straight. (Fig. 3-5)

图 3-5 鹤嘴手
Fig. 3-5 Crane's beak

6.单指   Single finger

食指伸直，其余四指的第一、二节指骨向内紧屈。（图3-6）

Keep the index finger straight, and bend the first and second segments of the remaining four fingers inward. (Fig. 3-6)

图 3-6 单指
Fig. 3-6 Single finger

二、步　型　　　　　　　　　　　　　　　　　Step Forms

1. 马步　　　　　　　　　　　　　　　　Mabu (Horse stance)

　　两脚分开，距离约为三倍脚长，脚尖正对前方，屈膝半蹲，膝关节不超过脚尖，上身正直，收腹敛臀，两手握拳置于腰两侧。（图3-7）

Stand with the feet apart. Make the distance about three times the length of the foot. Toes face straight forward. Do a half squat by bending the knees that do not track over the middle toe. Keep the upper body upright, draw in belly and hold back buttocks, and bring wrists against the waist with fingers curled inwards as f sts. (Fig. 3-7)

图 3-7　马步
Fig. 3-7 Horse stance

2. 弓步   Gongbu (Bow stance)

两脚前后分开，距离约为三倍脚长。一腿脚尖内扣，斜向前方，屈膝半蹲，膝关节与脚背在一条直线上；另一腿挺膝伸直，脚尖里扣；两脚全脚掌贴地。（图3-8）

Take a big step forward. The distance between the feet is about three times the length of the foot. For one leg, the toes face inward, and the leg face obliquely forward. Bend the knee and do a half squat, keeping the knee joint aligned with the instep. For another leg, straighten the knee and make the toes face inward. Keep soles of both feet on the ground. (Fig. 3-8)

图 3-8 弓步
Fig. 3-8 Bow stance

3. 虚步   Xubu (Empty stance)

虚步又名吊马。以左虚步为例，左腿微屈前伸，前脚掌虚点地面；右腿屈膝半蹲，脚尖斜向前方；收腹敛臀，重心落于右腿。（图3-9）

Empty stance is also known as diaoma (suspending the horse). Take the left empty step as an example, the left leg is slightly bent forward, and the forefoot slightly touches the ground; bend the right leg and do a half squat with the toes facing obliquely forward; draw in belly and hold back buttocks; put weight on the right leg. (Fig. 3-9)

图 3-9　虚步
Fig. 3-9　Empty stance

4. 拐步 Guaibu (Cross-legged stance)

两腿前后交叉。一腿屈膝下蹲，脚尖外展（约90°）；另一腿屈膝下跪，膝关节接近地面，脚跟离地；收腹敛臀。（图3-10）

Cross legs back and forth. The front leg bends under the knee with the toes moving outward (for about 90°); the knee of the other leg goes down to be close to the ground without touching it, the heel off the ground; draw in belly and hold back buttocks. (Fig. 3-10)

图 3-10　拐步
Fig. 3-10　Cross-legged stance

5. 骑龙步　　　　　　　　　　　　　　　Qilongbu (Dragon-riding stance)

一腿屈膝半蹲，全脚掌贴地；另一腿屈膝下跪（不得贴地），前脚掌贴地。两脚间相距约为三倍脚长。（图3-11）

Bend one knee into a half squat, the whole sole on the ground; raise the heel of the other leg, the forefoot on the ground and the knee close to the ground but not touching it. The distance between feet is about three times the length of foot. (Fig. 3-11)

图 3-11　骑龙步
Fig. 3-11 Dragon-riding stance

6. 跪步　　　　　　　　　　　　　　　　Guibu (Kneeling stance)

两脚前后分开，距离为两倍脚长。一腿屈膝下蹲；另一腿屈膝下跪，膝关节接近地面（不得贴地），脚跟离地；臀部后坐。（图3-12）

Stand with the feet apart. The distance between the front and back feet is about twice the length of the foot. One leg is fully bent, the other kneels down close to but not on the ground. The heel is raised from the ground, hips sitting on the heel. (Fig. 3-12)

图 3-12　跪步
Fig. 3-12　Kneeling stance

7. 半马步　　　　　　　　　　　　Banmabu (Half horse stance)

两脚左右分开，距离为二倍至三倍脚长。屈膝半蹲；右脚脚尖向前，左脚脚尖向左前方，重心偏于右腿（如右脚脚尖向右前方，则重心偏于左腿）；收腹敛臀。（图3-13）

Stand with the feet two-to-three-feet-length apart. Bend knees into a half squat, toes of the right foot facing forward, toes of the left foot facing front left. Put more weight on the right leg (When toes of the right foot facing front right, put more weight on the left leg). Draw in belly and hold back buttocks. (Fig. 3-13)

图 3-13　半马步
Fig. 3-13　Half horse stance

8. 独立步   Dulibu (Single-leg stance)

一腿站立支撑，另一腿屈膝提起，脚面绷直，脚尖向下内扣；收腹立腰，站立要稳。（图3-14）

Stand on one leg for support, bend the knee of the other leg and lift it, with the instep of the feet straight, and the toes pointing downwards. Draw in belly keep the back straight and stand firm. (Fig. 3-14)

图 3-14 独立步
Fig. 3-14 Single-leg stance

9. 单蝶步   Dandiebu (Single fold stance)

一腿屈膝下蹲，另一腿跪地（小腿内侧贴地）；收腹立腰。（图3-15）

Squat down with one knee bent, kneeling on the ground with the other knee (the inner calf on the ground). Draw in belly and keep the back straight. (Fig. 3-15)

图 3-15 单蝶步
Fig. 3-15 Single fold stance

南拳动作技法

Nan Quan Techniques

一、手 法   Hand Techniques

1. 拳法   Fist techniques

（1）冲拳：拳从腰间旋转，快速冲出，直臂或微屈臂，力达拳面。
（图4-1）

Chongquan (Thrust fist): The fist rotates from the waist, and rushes out quickly. Straighten the arm or bend it slightly, the strength reaching the fist face. (Fig. 4-1)

图 4-1　冲拳
Fig. 4-1 Thrust fist

（2）撞拳：肘微屈，肌肉紧张，短促用力向前撞出，力达拳面。
（图4-2）

Zhuangquan (Bump fist): The elbows are slightly bent, the muscles are tense, and the strength is exerted quickly and pushed forward for a "bump", reaching the fist face. (Fig. 4-2)

图 4-2　撞拳
Fig. 4-2 Bump fist

（3）盖拳：拳自上而下呈弧形运动，臂微屈，力达拳心。（图4-3）

Gaiquan (Thrust down fist): The fist moves like an arc from top to bottom, the arms are slightly bent, and the strength reaches the fist center. (Fig. 4-3)

图 4-3　盖拳
Fig. 4-3 Thrust down fist

（4）抛拳：拳自下而上呈环形运动，臂微屈，力达拳眼。（图4-4）

Paoquan (Throw fist): The fist moves in a circular motion from bottom to top, the arms are slightly bent, and the strength reaches the fist eye. (Fig. 4-4)

图 4-4　抛拳
Fig. 4-4 Throw fist

（5）挂拳：拳自上向下快速扣击，力达拳背。（图4-5）

Guaquan (Hang fist): The fist slams quickly from top to bottom, the strength reaching the back of the fist. (Fig. 4-5)

图 4-5　挂拳
Fig. 4-5 Hang fist

（6）鞭拳：手臂由屈到伸，向侧面鞭击，力达拳背。（图4-6）

Bianquan (Whip fist): Extend the arm from its bending position, whip to the side, the strength reaching the back of the fist. (Fig. 4-6)

图 4-6　鞭拳
Fig. 4-6 Whip fist

2. 掌法　　　　　　　　　　　　　　　　　　　　Palm techniques

（1）推掌：掌从腰间短促有力向前推出，直臂或微屈臂，力达掌根或掌外沿。（图4-7）

Push palm: Push the palm straight forward from the waist with a burst of strength, the arm straight or slightly bent. Convey the strength to the palm root or the outer side. (Fig. 4-7)

图 4-7　推掌
Fig. 4-7 Push palm

（2）挑掌：单掌或两掌，由内向外挑出，上臂与前臂夹角约90°，指尖向斜前上方，力达前臂外侧。（图4-8）

Tiaozhang (Stick up palm): Stick up palm or palms outward from the inside out. The angle between the upper arm and the forearm is about 90°. Fingertips face obliquely upward. Convey the strength to the outside of the forearm(s). (Fig. 4-8)

图 4-8　挑掌
Fig. 4-8 Stick up palm

（3）标掌：单掌或两掌，短促有力前插，力达指尖。（图4-9）

Biaozhang [Thrust palm(s) forward]: Thrust palm(s) straight forward quickly and forcefully. The strength reaches fintertips. (Fig. 4-9)

图 4-9　标掌
Fig. 4-9 Thrust palm(s) forward

（4）盘手双推掌：两拳变掌，从左向上经脸前向右盘手，左掌置于右胸前，掌心向右，掌指向上；右掌置于右腰侧，掌心向前，掌指向下。目视左侧。

两掌同时向左侧平推，两肘微屈；左掌心向下，右掌心向上，掌指均向右，小指侧成横线，与胸平高。目视两掌。（图4-10）

Push palms in a winding hand position: Change fists into palms. Move the hands in a winding path from upside through the front of the face to the right. Put the left palm in front of the right side of the chest, with the palm center facing right and palm fingers facing upward. Place the right palm to the right side of the waist, with the palm center facing forward and the palm fingers facing downward. Look left.

Push both palms to the left horizontally at the same time, elbows slightly bent. The left palm faces downward and the right one faces upward, all palm fingers facing right. Make the little finger sides into a horizontal line at chest height. Look at both palms. (Fig. 4-10)

图 4-10　盘手双推掌
Fig. 4-10　Push palms in a winding hand position

3. 爪法 Claw techniques

（1）抓面爪：拳变虎爪，由腰间向前抓击，手心向前，与面平高，力达指端。（图4-11）

Scratch-face claw: Change the fist into a tiger claw and make a scratching strike forward from the waist, with the claw center facing forward at face height. Convey the strength to fingertips. (Fig. 4-11)

图 4-11　抓面爪
Fig. 4-11 Scratch-face claw

（2）鹤嘴手（前啄）：掌变鹤嘴手，向前上方短促用力啄击，力达指端。（图4-12）

Crane's beak (pecking forward): Change the palm into a crane's beak and pecks upward to the front by exerting short strength. Convey the strength to fingertips. (Fig. 4-12)

图 4-12　鹤嘴手（前啄）
Fig. 4-12 Crane's beak (pecking forward)

4.肘法 Elbow techniques

（1）撞肘：握拳、屈肘，用肘尖顶击，力达肘尖。（图4-13）

Bump elbow: Make a fist and bend the elbow. Make a bumping strike with the tip of the elbow where the strength reaches. (Fig. 4-13)

图 4-13 撞肘
Fig. 4-13 Bump elbow

（2）压肘：屈臂，抬肘经胸前向异侧反臂下压，力达肘尖。（图 4-14）

Press elbow: Bend the arm, raise the elbow and press it down on the cpposite side of the arm through the chest. Convey the strength to the tip of the elbow. (Fig. 4-14)

图 4-14 压肘
Fig. 4-14 Press elbow

（3）担肘：屈臂，肘由下向上抬，力达肘尖。（图4-15）

Lift elbow: Bend the arm and lift up the elbow from below. Convey the strength to the tip of the elbow. (Fig. 4-15)

图 4-15 担肘
Fig. 4-15 Lift elbow

5. 桥法　　　　　　　　　　　　　　　　"Bridge" techniques

（1）圈桥：臂侧伸，以肘关节为轴，前臂由外向内沿立圆圈绕。（图4-16）

Quanqiao (Move around the "bridge"): Extend the arm sideways. Taking the elbow joint as the axis, move the forearm from the outside to the inside along a vertical circle. (Fig. 4-16)

图 4-16 圈桥
Fig. 4-16 Move around the "bridge"

（2）缠桥：以左手缠桥为例，左臂侧伸，以手腕为轴由外向内立圆缠拿。（图4-17）

Chanqiao (Twine "bridge"): Take chanqiao with the left hand as an example. The left arm stretches to the side, twine and catch around a vertical circle from the outside to the inside by using the elbow joint as the axis. (Fig. 4-17)

图 4-17　缠桥
Fig. 4-17　Twine "bridge"

（3）盘桥：屈臂或臂微屈立圆绕圈，高不过头，低不过裆。（图4-18）

Panqiao (Circle around "bridge"): Bend or slightly bend arms and move them around a vertical circle, not higher than the head nor lower than the scotch. (Fig. 4-18)

图 4-18　盘桥
Fig. 4-18　Circle around "bridge"

（4）沉桥：屈肘使前臂由上向下挫沉，力达前臂。（图4-19）

Chenqiao (Sink "bridge"): Bend arms and sink forearms down from above. Convey strength to forearms. (Fig. 4-19)

图 4-19　沉桥
Fig. 4-19 Sink "bridge"

（5）劈桥：前臂用力向下猛劈，力达前臂。（图4-20）

Piqiao (Chop "bridge"): Chop down hard with the forearm where the strength reaches. (Fig. 4-20)

图 4-20　劈桥
Fig. 4-20 Chop "bridge"

（6）攻桥：肘微屈，前臂内旋向前横击，力达掌外沿。（图4-21）

Gongqiao (Attack "bridge"): Slightly bend elbows. Rotate the forearm inward and make a horizontal strike. Convey strength to the outside of the palm. (Fig. 4-21)

图 4-21　攻桥
Fig. 4-21 Attack "bridge"

（7）截桥：臂微屈，前臂外旋或内旋，向下、左、右截击。（图4-22）

Jieqiao (Cut "bridge"): Slightly bend arms. Rotate forearms outward or inward. Cut to the downside, left side and right side. (Fig. 4-22)

图 4-22　截桥
Fig. 4-22 Cut "bridge"

（8）架桥：屈肘，前臂斜横架于头前上方，力达前臂外侧。（图 4-23）

Jiaqiao (Build "bridge"): Bend elbows. Place the forearms diagonally above the head. Convey the strength to the outside of forearms. (Fig. 4-23)

图 4-23　架桥
Fig. 4-23　Build "bridge"

（9）穿桥：一掌从另一臂的下方紧贴向前穿出，腕外展。（图4-24）

Chuanqiao (Cross "bridge"): A palm goes out from the underside of the other arm, the wrist turning outward. (Fig. 4-24)

图 4-24　穿桥
Fig. 4-24　Cross "bridge"

二、步 法 Step Position

1. 上步 Step forward

一脚经另一脚内侧向前迈步。（图4-25）

Step forward with one foot through the inside of the other foot. (Fig. 4-25)

图 4-25　上步
Fig. 4-25　Step forward

2. 退步 Step backward

一脚经另一脚内侧向后退步。（图4-26）

Step backward with one foot through the inside of the other foot. (Fig. 4-26)

图 4-26　退步
Fig. 4-26　Step backward

3. 拖步   Tuobu (Take a dragging step)

一脚向前跨大步，另一脚拖地跟一小步。（图4-27）

Take a big step forward with one foot, and make a small dragging step with the other foot to follow. (Fig. 4-27)

图 4-27　拖步
Fig. 4-27 Take a dragging step

4. 盖步   Gaibu (Forward-inserting step)

一脚经另一脚脚前横迈步，全脚掌贴地，脚尖外展，两腿交叉。（图4-28）

Step laterally with one foot in front of the other, with the soles of the feet touching the ground, toes outstretched, and legs crossed. (Fig. 4-28)

图 4-28　盖步
Fig. 4-28 Forward-inserting step

5. 插步　　　　　　　　　　　　　　　　Chabu (Back cross-step)

一脚向另一脚的后方插步，前脚掌贴地，两腿交叉。（图4-29）

Step backward behind the other foot with one foot, the forefoot touching the ground, and the legs crossed. (Fig. 4-29)

图 4-29　插步
Fig. 4-29 Back cross-step

6. 走三角步　　　　　　　　　　　　　　　　　Triangle step

由并步开始，左脚向右前方上步，脚尖外展，膝微屈；右腿屈膝下跪，脚跟离地。右脚由后经左脚前绕上一步，脚尖内扣，左脚脚跟离地，两腿微屈。身体左转，左脚弧形后退一步，转身成马步或半马步。（图4-30）

Start with the feet-together stance, and then step forward to the right with the left foot, toes stretching out and the knee slightly bend. Bend the right leg and kneel down, with the heel off the ground. Take a step forward with the right foot from the back through the front of the left foot, toes facing inward, the left heel off the ground, and both legs slightly bent. Turn left, step back in an arc shape with the left foot, and turn round to form a horse or half horse stance. (Fig. 4-30)

图 4-30　走三角步
Fig. 4-30 Triangle step

7. 麒麟步　　　　　　　　　　　　　　　　　　　　　　　Qilin step

左、右脚连续向右、左前方上步，形成两次拐步。（图4-31）

Step up to the right and left front with the left and right foot in succession, forming two cross-legged steps. (Fig. 4-31)

图 4-31　麒麟步
Fig. 4-31 Qilin step

三、腿 法   Leg Techniques

1. 前蹬腿   Front kick with heel

身体直立，腿由屈到伸，脚尖翘起，向前蹬击，力达脚跟。（图4-32）

Keep the body upright. Extend the leg from its bending position, lift toes up and make a kicking strike forward. Convey strength to the heel. (Fig. 4-32)

图 4-32　前蹬腿
Fig. 4-32　Front kick with heel

2. 前钉腿   Front leg nailing

一腿屈膝支撑，另一腿提起由屈到伸，迅速向前下方钉踢，脚尖绷直，高不过膝，力达脚尖。（图4-33）

Bend one leg for support, lift the other one, extend it from its bending position, and quickly kick forward to the downside, with the toes straight, and not higher than the knee. Convey the strength to the toes. (Fig. 4-33)

图 4-33　前钉腿
Fig. 4-33 Front leg nailing

3. 踩腿 {style="display:inline"}　　　　　　　　　　　　　　　　Step down with leg

一腿屈膝支撑，另一腿提膝外展，由屈到伸，迅速向前下方踩出，脚尖向外勾紧，高不过膝，力达脚弓内侧。（图4-34）

Bend one leg for support, and raise the knee of the other leg and turn it outward. Step forward to the downside quickly after extending the leg from its bending position, the toes tightly hooked, facing outward and not higher than the knee. The strength reaches the inner side of the arch of the foot. (Fig. 4-34)

图 4-34　踩腿
Fig. 4-34 Step down with leg

4. 侧踹腿   Side kick with sole leading

一腿支撑，另一腿提膝，脚尖勾起，由屈到伸，向体侧踹出，力达脚跟，上体倾斜。（图4-35）

Use one leg for support. Lift the toes of the other leg, and kick out from flexion to extension to the side of the body. The strength reaches the heel. The upper body leans forward. (Fig. 4-35)

图 4-35　侧踹腿
Fig. 4-35　Side kick with sole leading

5. 横钉腿   Side leg nailing

一腿支撑，另一腿提膝，脚尖勾起，由屈到伸，向异侧钉击，力达前脚掌。（图4-36）

Use one leg for support. Lift the toes of the other leg, extend the leg from its bending position, and make a nailing strike to the other side of the body. Convey strength to the forefoot. (Fig. 4-36)

图 4-36　横钉腿
Fig. 4-36　Side leg nailing

南拳段前九级考评技术内容

A Nine-tier Pre-Duan Grading System for Nan Quan

南拳段前一级　　　　　　　Nan Quan: Pre-Duan Level 1

（一）掌法 + 拳法 + 爪法 + 平衡 + 步型 + 步法
Techniques of Palm+Fist+Claw+Balance+Step form+Step position

1. 预备势　　　　　　　　　　　　　　　　Preparatory posture

两脚并步，直腿站立，直臂两掌贴靠于两腿外侧；两掌握拳提抱于腰间，拳心向上；目视前方。（图5-1）

要点：挺胸、收腹、敛臀，提神降气。

Stand with the feet together, legs straight, arms straight, and both palms against the outside of the legs; clench both hands into fists, and then raise them around the waist, the fist centers up; look straight ahead. (Fig. 5-1)

Key points: Thrust chest forward, draw in belly, hold back buttocks, keep spirits up and lower the qi.

图 5-1　预备势
Fig. 5-1 Preparatory posture

2. 马步盖掌   Thump palm in a horse stance

左脚向左侧开步成马步，同时腰微右转；左拳变掌由左侧经面前盖至右胸前，掌心向右；目视前方。（图5-2）

要点：马步沉稳，脚跟不可离地，屈蹲腿不可低于水平位；马步、盖掌同一时间完成，动作过程中手眼配合紧密。

Step to the left side with the left foot and form a horse stance. At the same time, turn the waist slightly to the right, change the left fist into a palm, and thump it from the left side through the front to the right side of the chest, with the palm facing right. Look straight ahead. (Fig. 5-2)

Key points: Keep the horse stance steady, heels on the ground, and squatting legs not lower than the horizontal position; the horse stance and palm thumping should be completed at the same time, and the hands and eyes should be well coordinated.

图 5-2　马步盖掌
Fig. 5-2 Thump palm in a horse stance

3. 马步左右冲拳　　　　　　　Thrust fist left and right in a horse stance

马步不动，左掌变拳收至腰间，右拳向前冲出，拳心向下；右拳收至腰间，左拳向前冲出，拳心向下；目视前方。（图5-3）

要点：马步沉稳，冲拳时力发于腰，力达拳面，冲拳与收拳须一致，劲力充沛。

Stay in a horse stance, turn the left palm into a fist and withdraw it to the waist. Thrust the right fist forward, the fist center facing downward. Draw the right fist back to the waist, and thrust the left fist forward, with the fist center facing downward. Look straight ahead. (Fig. 5-3)

Key points: Keep the horse stance steady; when thrusting, exert strength from the waist; convey the strength to the surface of the fist; fist thrusting and withdrawing should be powerfully done at the same time.

图 5-3　马步左右冲拳
Fig. 5-3 Thrust fist left and right in a horse stance

4. 独立步虎爪　　　　　　　　　　　Tiger claw on a single foot

两拳变掌，屈肘收于腰侧成左侧蝶掌；右脚提起成独立步，同时两掌变虎爪向右前方推出，两臂相距20～30厘米；目视前方。（图5-4）

要点：独立步保持稳定，提膝要高于腰部，提起腿脚须内扣；虎爪推出时结合转腰发力，五指用力张开，掌心凸出，两臂刚劲有力。

Change both fists into palms, bend the elbows, draw them back to the waist side, and form the left-sided butterfly palm; lift the right foot and stand on the left one when changing both palms into tiger claws and pushing them to the right frond side with a 20-30 cm distance between the arms. Look straight ahead. (Fig. 5-4)

Key points: Keep it steady when standing on a single foot. The knee should be above the waist, and the foot should be bent downward at the ankle when lifting the leg. When the tiger claws are pushed out, turn the waist to exert strength. The five fingers are stretched out, the palm is protruding, and the arms are strong and powerful.

图 5-4　独立步虎爪
Fig. 5-4 Tiger claw on a single foot

（二）爪法 + 桥法 + 步法
Techniques of Claw+Bridge+Step position

1. 预备势   Preparatory posture

两脚并步，直腿站立，直臂两掌贴靠于两腿外侧；两掌握拳提抱于腰间，拳心向上；目视前方。（图5-5）

要点：挺胸、收腹、敛臀，提神降气。

Stand with the feet together, legs straight, arms straight, and both palms against the outside of the legs; clench both hands to form fists, and then raise them around the waist, the fist centers up; look straight ahead. (Fig. 5-5)

Key points: Thrust chest forward, draw in belly, hold back buttocks, keep spirits up and lower the qi.

图 5-5　预备势
Fig. 5-5 Preparatory posture

2.并步穿桥   Cross "bridge" in a feet-together stance

两脚并步站立；左拳变掌沿右臂下向前穿出，掌心由向下变斜向前，掌指向左；右拳收至腰间，拳心向上；目视前方。（图5-6）

要点：穿桥时注意左穿右拉，拧腰旋臂，穿桥与右拳回收要一致，腰微向右转，对称拧转。

Stand with the feet together. The left fist turns into a palm and goes forward from under the right arm like crossing a bridge. The palm changes from facing downward to obliquely forward, fingers facing to the left. Draw back the right fist to the waist with the fist center facing upward. Look straight ahead. (Fig. 5-6)

Key points: When crossing a "bridge", the left palm crosses, and the right one pulls. Twist the waist and rotate the right arm. Cross the bridge and withdraw the right fist at the same time. Turn the waist slightly to the right side. The reverse twist action is the same.

图 5-6　并步穿桥
Fig. 5-6 Cross "bridge" in a feet-together stance

3. 俯身虎爪　　　　　　Tiger claw in a body-bending-forward position

左脚向左前方上步，脚跟贴地，脚尖勾起；同时右拳变虎爪向左下方推出，左拳收抱于腰间，拳心向上；目视右虎爪。（图5-7）

要点：俯身向下推出时尽量向前，牵拉腿部韧带；虎爪五指用力张开，掌心凸出；精神饱满，寓猛虎下山之意。

Step up forward with the left foot to the left, with heels on the ground, and toes raised; at the same time, the right fist changes into a tiger claw and pushes out to the lower left, and the left fist is withdrawn around the waist, with the fist center facing upward; look at the right tiger claw. (Fig. 5-7)

Key points: When the body bends forward, try to push out the right claw as far as possible, pulling the ligaments of the legs. The five fingers of the tiger's claw are stretched out, the palm protruding. Be full of spirit and energy, which implies the tiger comes down the mountain.

图 5-7　俯身虎爪
Fig. 5-7 Tiger claw in a body-bending-forward position

南拳段前二级 　　　　Nan Quan: Pre-Duan Level 2

南拳段前二级
Nan Quan: Pre-
Duan Level 2

（一）掌法＋拳法＋指法＋步型＋步法
Techniques of Palm+Fist+Finger+Step form+Step position

1. 预备势 　　　　　　　　　　　　　　Preparatory posture

两脚并步，直腿站立，直臂两掌贴靠于两腿外侧；两掌握拳提抱于腰间，拳心向上；目视前方。（图5-8）

要点：挺胸、收腹、敛臀，提神降气。

Stand with the feet together, legs straight, arms straight, and both palms against the outside of the legs; clench both hands into fists, and then raise them around the waist, the fist centers up; look straight ahead. (Fig. 5-8)

Key points: Thrust chest forward, draw in belly, hold back buttocks, keep spirits up and lower the qi.

图 5-8　预备势
Fig. 5-8 Preparatory posture

2. 虚步冲拳推掌　　　　　　　Push palm and thrust fist in an empty stance

右脚向右前方上步，右拳提至右胸前，拳心向下；左拳变掌摆至右胸前，掌心与右拳面相对；左脚移动成左虚步，同时右拳与左掌向前冲拳、推掌，两臂伸直与肩同高、同宽；目视前方。（图5-9）

要点：步法移动时重心下沉；虚步重心在右腿，虚实分明；冲拳、推掌发力于腰，眼随手动。

Step forward to the right side with the right foot, raise the right fist to the front of the right side of the chest, with the fist center facing downward. Change the left fist into a palm and swing it to front of the right side of the chest, with the palm center facing the right fist surface. Move the left foot into a left empty stance, while thrusting the right fist and pushing the left palm forward, with arms kept straight at shoulder height and shoulder-width apart. Look straight ahead. (Fig. 5-9)

Key points: When changing the step position, move the center of gravity downward. The weight is on the right leg in an empty stance. Differentiate between "Xu" and "Shi" (Make clear of empty and solid movements). Exert strength from the waist when thrusting fist and pushing palm, eyes following the movement of hands.

图 5-9　虚步冲拳推掌
Fig. 5-9 Push palm and thrust fist in an empty stance

3. 马步双切掌　　　　　　　　Double-palm cutting in a horse stance

左脚向左移动成马步，右拳变掌，两掌收至左腰侧，两掌心均向上；两掌以小指侧为力点同时向前攻出，右掌与胸同高，左掌与腹同高，掌心均向下；目视前方。（图5-10）

要点：马步沉稳，脚跟不可离地；双切掌时以腰带臂，发力于腰，动作过程中手眼配合紧密。

Step to the left with the left foot and form a horse stance, with both palms withdrawn to the left side of the waist and both palms facing upward; use the sides of both little fingers to exent strength and push them forward at the same time. The right palm is at chest height, and the left palm at belly height, both palms facing downward. Look straight ahead. (Fig. 5-10)

Key points: Keep the horse stance stable, heels on the ground. Exert strength from the waist in the double-palm cutting, and use the waist to drive arms. Keep a good hand-eye coordination.

图 5-10　马步双切掌
Fig. 5-10 Double-palm cutting in a horse stance

4. 马步双推指　　　　　　　　Double-finger pushing in a horse stance

　　马步不动，左掌由下经右臂内侧弧形挑至左肩前，右掌经外向下沿左臂内侧弧形挑至右肩前，掌指均向上；两掌变单指手，两臂屈肘挑至两肩上，两手心斜向上，两掌收至腰侧，用劲慢慢向前推出，臂与肩平；目视前方。（图5-11）

　　要点：马步沉稳，脚跟不可离地；双推指推出时，沉肘、坐腕、翘指，两臂刚劲有力，动作过程中手眼配合紧密。

Stay in a horse stance. Lift the left palm in an arc from the bottom through the inner side of the right arm to the front of the left shoulder, and raise the right palm from the outside to the inside of the left arm in an arc to the front of the right shoulder, both palm fingers facing upward. Change both palms into the single-finger position, bend the arms and lift elbows, fingers standing on both shoulders and palms facing obliquely upward. Then draw the two fingers back to the waist sides, and slowly push them forward. Keep arms at shoulder height, and look straight ahead. (Fig. 5-11)

Key points: Keep the horse stance stable, heels on the ground. When pushing the two fingers, drop elbows, lower the wrists and keep the two fingers upright. Keep arms strong and have a good hand-eye coordination.

图 5-11　马步双推指
Fig. 5-11 Double-finger pushing in a horse stance

（二）掌法＋拳法＋腿法＋步型＋步法
Techniques of Palm+Fist+Leg+Step form+Step position

1. 预备势　　　　　　　　　　　　　　　Preparatory posture

两脚并步，直腿站立，直臂两掌贴靠于两腿外侧；两掌握拳提抱于腰间，拳心向上；目视前方。（图5-12）

要点：挺胸、收腹、敛臀，提神降气。

Stand with the feet together, legs straight, arms straight, and both palms against the outside of the legs; clench both hands to form fists, and then raise them around the waist, the fist centers up; look straight ahead. (Fig. 5-12)

Key points: Thrust chest forward, draw in belly, hold back buttocks, keep spirits up and lower the qi.

图 5-12　预备势
Fig. 5-12　Preparatory posture

2. 右弓步蝶掌   Butterfly palm in a right bow stance

右脚向前成右弓步，左腿伸直，左脚全脚掌贴地；两掌向前推出，右掌在上，掌指向上，左掌在下，掌指向下，两掌相距20～30厘米；目视前方。（图5-13）

要点：弓步时，右膝垂直于脚背；推掌时，要蹬脚、扣膝、拧腰转髋发力；发力时，上下肢协调一致，力发于根。

Step forward with the right foot into a right bow stance. Keep the left leg straight, and the whole sole of the left foot on the ground. Push both palms forward, with the right palm on the top, the fingers facing upward, and the left palm on the bottom, the fingers facing downward. The distance between the two palms is 20-30 cm. Look straight ahead. (Fig. 5-13)

Key points: Keep the right knee perpendicular to the instep in the bow stance. When pushing the palms, kick with heel, twist the knees, turn the waist and hips to exert strength. The upper and lower limbs should be well coordinated in strength exertion. The strength comes from the root, i.e. the feet.

图 5-13　右弓步蝶掌
Fig. 5-13 Butterfly palm in a right bow stance

3. 左弓步冲拳 · Thrust fist in a left bow stance

左脚向前成左弓步，右腿伸直，右脚全脚掌贴地；两掌变拳，左拳收至腰间，右拳直线向前冲出，拳心向下；目视前方。（图5-14）

要点：弓步时，左膝垂直于脚背；冲拳时，力起于根（右脚），拧腰转髋发力，力达拳面；发力时，上下肢协调一致。

Step forward with the left foot into a left bow stance. Keep the right leg straight, and the whole sole of the right foot on the ground. Draw the left fist back to the waist, and thrust the right fist forward in a straight line, with the fist center facing downward. Look straight ahead. (Fig. 5-14)

Key points: Keep the left knee perpendicular to the instep in the bow stance. When thrusting fist, exert strength from the root (the right foot). Exert strength when twisting the waist and turning hips. Convey the strength to the fist surface. The upper and lower limbs should be well coordinated in strength exertion.

图 5-14　左弓步冲拳
Fig. 5-14 Thrust fist in a left bow stance

4. 单拍脚马步侧冲拳
One-foot-slap and side-fist-thrust in a horse stance

右腿挺直向上摆动，同时左拳变掌拍击右脚脚面，右拳收抱于腰间；右腿下落顺势成马步，同时左掌屈肘收至右胸前，右拳随转体向右侧冲出，拳眼向上；目视右拳。（图5-15）

要点：马步沉稳，脚跟不可离地，屈蹲腿不可低于水平位；右脚落步与转体冲拳一致，冲拳发力于腰。

The right leg swings straight up, and at the same time, the left fist turns into the palm and slaps the top of the right foot. The right fist is drawn back to the waist. Drop the right leg into a horse stance while bending the elbow and drawing the left palm to the front of the right side of the chest. Thrust the right fist to the right side when turning right, with the fist eye facing upward. Look at the right fist. (Fig. 5-15)

Key points: Keep the horse stance stable, heels on the ground. The squatting leg should not be lower than the horizontal level. Right foot landing should be done simultaneously with fist thrusting. Exert strength from the waist when thrusting.

图 5-15　单拍脚马步侧冲拳
Fig. 5-15　One-foot-slap and side-fist-thrust in a horse stance

南拳段前三级   Nan Quan: Pre-Duan Level 3

南拳段前三级
Nan Quan: Pre-
Duan Level 3

（一）掌法＋拳法＋腿法＋步型＋步法
Techniques of Palm+Fist+Leg+Step form+Step position

1. 预备势   Preparatcry posture

两脚并步，直腿站立，直臂两掌贴靠于两腿外侧；两掌握拳提抱于腰间，拳心向上；目视前方。（图5-16）

要点：挺胸、收腹、敛臀，提神降气。

Stand with the feet together, legs straight, arms straight, and both palms against the outside of the legs; clench both hands into fists, and then raise them around the waist, the fist centers up; look straight ahead. (Fig. 5-16)

Key points: Thrust chest forward, draw in belly, hold back buttocks, keep spirits up and lower the qi.

图 5-16 预备势
Fig. 5-16 Preparatory posture

2.马步双冲拳   Thrust both fists in a horse stance

左脚向左开步成马步，同时两拳斜向下方正面冲出，拳心向下，两臂与腹同高、与肩同宽；目视前方。（图5-17）

要点：脚跟不可离地；冲拳时腰先微右转，以腰发力，力达拳面。

Step to the left with the left foot and form a horse stance. At the same time, thrust both fists obliquely downward, with fist centers facing downward. Keep the arms at belly hight and should-width apart. Look straight ahead. (Fig. 5-17)

Key points: Keep heels on the ground. When thrusting fists, turn the waist slightly to the right, exert strength from the waist, and convey the strength to the fist surfaces.

图 5-17　马步双冲拳
Fig. 5-17 Thrust both fists in a horse stance

3. 马步挑掌沉桥　　　　Stick up palm and sink "bridge" in a horse stance

马步不动，两拳变掌随屈臂经下向里分挑至两肩前，沉肩垂肘，两前臂内旋下沉与腹部同高；目视前方。（图5-18）

要点：马步沉稳，脚跟不可离地；挑掌和沉桥均以肘关节为轴，夹腋沉肘，动作幅度宜小。

Stay in a horse stance. Change fists into palms which follow the bending of the arms. Lift palms inward to the front of the two shoulders. Lower shoulders and elbows. Rotate both forearms inward and lower them to the height of the belly. Look straight ahead. (Fig. 5-18)

Key points: Keep the horse stance stable, heels on the ground. Take the elbow joint as the axis when sticking up palms and sinking "bridge" (arms), armpits clamped, and elbows lowered. Keep the range of movements small.

图 5-18　马步挑掌沉桥
Fig. 5-18 Stick up palm and sink "bridge" in a horse stance

4. 马步标掌沉桥　　　Thrust palms and sink "bridge" in a horse stance

马步不动，两臂屈肘，两掌变指挑至肩上；两肘下沉，两指收至腰间；两指变掌快速向前标出，掌心相对；两前臂快速下沉，垂肘翘指；目视前方。（图5-19）

要点：动作过程中马步保持沉稳，标掌要快速有爆发劲，沉桥时用劲短促，力达前臂尺骨侧。

Stay in a horse stance. Bend the elbows, remain two fingers of the palms and lift them to the shoulders. Lower the elbows, and draw the two fingers back to the waist. Then change them back to palms and thrust them forward quickly, with the palms facing each other. Make the forearms sink quickly, lower elbows and keep fingers upright. Look straight ahead. (Fig. 5-19)

Key points: Keep the horse stance stable in movements. Be quick and explosive at palm thrusting. Make "jin" (strength) short when sinking the "bridge". Convey the strength to the ulnar side of the forearms.

图 5-19　马步标掌沉桥
Fig. 5-19 Thrust palms and sink "bridge" in a horse stance

5. 右弓步架打

Strike out one fist with the other upheld in a right bow stance

右脚向右前迈出，左腿伸直，成右弓步，左脚全脚掌贴地；同时右拳上架于头前上方，左拳向前平冲，拳眼向上；目视左拳。（图5-20）

要点：弓步时右膝垂直于脚背；架打时要蹬脚、扣膝、合胯，拧腰转髋发力，力发于根。

Step forward with the right foot into a bow stance, the left leg straight, and all the left foot on the ground. At the same time, place the right fist above the head, and strike out the left fist straight forward, with the fist eye facing upward. Look at the left fist. (Fig. 5-20)

Key points: Keep the right knee perpendicular to the instep in the bow stance. When striking out one fist, kick with heel, twist the knees, turn the waist and hips to exert strength. The strength comes from the root, i.e. the feet.

图 5-20　右弓步架打
Fig. 5-20 Strike out one fist with the other upheld in a right bow stance

（二）掌法＋拳法＋桥法＋步法＋步型
Techniques of Palm+Fist+Bridge+Step form+Step position

1.预备势   Preparatory posture

两脚并步，直腿站立，直臂两掌贴靠于两腿外侧；两掌握拳提抱于腰间，拳心向上；目视前方。（图5-21）

要点：挺胸、收腹、敛臀，提神降气。

Stand with the feet together, legs straight, arms straight, and both palms against the outside of the legs; clench both hands into fists, and then raise them around the waist, the fist centers up; look straight ahead. (Fig. 5-21)

Key points: Thrust chest forward, draw in belly, hold back buttocks, keep spirits up and lower the qi.

图 5-21　预备势
Fig. 5-21 Preparatory posture

2. 左骑龙步双推掌　　　　　　Push palms in a left dragon-riding stance

左脚向左前上步成半马步，两掌屈肘收抱于右侧成蝶掌；右脚跟步成左骑龙步，同时两掌向左前平推，左掌心向下，右掌心向上，掌指均向右；目视两掌。（图5-22）

要点：骑龙步时，右腿膝关节不要贴地；半马步时蓄劲，腰微右转；双推掌时，左臂成半圆，右肘下沉，发力于腰。

Step forward to the left with the left foot and form a half horse stance. Bend the elbows, draw back both palms to the right side, and form the butterfly palm. The right foot follows to make a left dragon-riding stance. At the same time, push both palms left forward, with the left palm facing downward, the right palm facing upward, and fingers facing to the right. Look at both palms. (Fig. 5-22)

Key points: The knee joint of the right leg should not touch the ground when forming the dragon-riding stance. Store up energy when forming the half horse stance. Turn the waist slightly to the right. When pushing palms, the left arm is formed into a semicircle, the right elbow is lowered, and the strength is exerted from the waist.

图 5-22　左骑龙步双推掌
Fig. 5-22 Push palms in a left dragon-riding stance

3. 右骑龙步双推掌　　　Push palms in a right dragon-riding stance

右脚向右前上步成半马步，两掌屈肘收抱于左侧成蝶掌；左脚跟步成右骑龙步，同时两掌向右前平推，右掌心向下，左掌心向上，掌指均向左；目视两掌。（图5-23）

要点：骑龙步时，左腿膝关节不要贴地；半马步时蓄劲，腰微左转；双推掌时，右臂成半圆，左肘下沉，发力于腰。

Step forward to the right with the right foot and form a half horse stance. Bend the elbows, draw back both palms to the left side, and form the butterfly palm. The left foot follows to make a right dragon-riding stance. At the same time, push both palms right forward, with the right palm facing downward, the left palm facing upward, and fingers facing to the left. Look at both palms. (Fig. 5-23)

Key points: The left knee joint should not touch the ground when forming the dragon-riding stance. Store up energy when making the half horse stance. Slightly turn the waist to the left. When pushing the palms, the right arm is form into a semicircle, the left elbow is lowered, and the strength is exerted from the waist.

图 5-23　右骑龙步双推掌
Fig. 5-23 Push palms in a right dragon-riding stance

4.骑龙步劈桥　　　　　　　Chop "bridge" in a dragon-riding stance

左脚向前成骑龙步，同时右臂外旋，以尺骨侧为力点经上向体前下劈，拳心向上；左掌由下向上摆至右上臂内侧，掌心向右；目视右拳。（图5-24）

要点：骑龙步时，右膝关节不要贴地；劈桥时右臂外旋，屈肘下沉。

Step forward with the left foot into a dragon-riding stance. At the same time, turn the right arm outward, and chop it down by exerting strength from the ulnar side, the fist center facing upward. Swing the left palm from bottom to top to the inside of the right upper arm, with the palm facing right. Look at the right fist. (Fig. 5-24)

Key points: The right knee joint should not touch the ground when forming the dragon-riding stance. When chopping the "bridge", swing the right arm outward and lower the right elbow.

图 5-24　骑龙步劈桥
Fig. 5-24 Chop "bridge" in a dragon-riding stance

南拳段前四级 — Nan Quan: Pre-Duan Level 4

南拳段前四级
Nan Quan: Pre-
Duan Level 4

（一）平衡＋腿法＋爪法＋桥法＋拳法＋步法＋步型
Techniques of Balance+Leg+Claw+Bridge+Fist+
Step form+Step position

1. 预备势   Preparatory posture

两脚并步，直腿站立，直臂两掌贴靠于两腿外侧；两掌握拳提抱于腰间，拳心向上；目视前方。（图5-25）

要点：挺胸、收腹、敛臀，提神降气。

Stand with the feet together, legs straight, arms straight, and both palms against the outside of the legs; clench both hands into fists, and then raise them around the waist, the fist centers up; look straight ahead. (Fig. 5-25)

Key points: Thrust chest forward, draw in belly, hold back buttocks, keep spirits up and lower the qi.

图 5-25　预备势
Fig. 5-25 Preparatory posture

2. 独立步左蹬脚　　　　　　　　Kick with left heel on a single foot

右脚向前上步，同时两拳变虎爪经头上交叉后摆至两侧；右腿伸直独立支撑，左腿屈膝抬起，向前蹬出；目视前方。（图5-26）

要点：支撑腿挺膝收髋，五趾抓地；蹬脚屈伸明显，挺膝勾脚，发力快脆，力达脚跟。

Step forward with the right foot, and at the same time, change both fists into tiger claws which cross over the head and then swing to the sides. Keep the right leg straight for independent support. Bend and raise the left leg. And then kick with heel forward. Look straight ahead. (Fig. 5-26)

Key points: Keep the supporting leg and the knee straight, retracting hips, and grabbing the ground with the five toes. Make the flexion and extension of the kick obvious, keeping the knee straight and turning the toes upward. Exert strength in a fast and smooth way. Convey the strength to the heel.

图 5-26　独立步左蹬脚
Fig. 5-26　Kick with left heel on a single foot

3. 跪步推爪　　　　　　　　　　　Push claw in a kneeling stance

左脚向前落步成半马步，右虎爪收至腰间，左虎爪摆至体前，手心向前；右脚向前跟步成跪步，同时右虎爪向前推出，左虎爪收至右肘下内侧，手心向前；目视右虎爪。（图5-27）

要点：跪步时膝关节不要触及地面，臀部要坐在下跪腿小腿上；左脚落步与左虎爪下按一致，推右虎爪时发力于腰。

Step forward with the left foot into a half horse stance. Withdraw the right tiger claw to the waist, and place the left tiger claw in front of the body, the claw center facing forward. Step forward with the right leg into a kneeling stance, and at the same time push the right tiger claw forward. Draw the left tiger claw to the inner side of the right elbow, the claw center facing forward. Look at the right tiger claw. (Fig. 5-27)

Key points: The knee joint should not touch the ground in the kneeling stance, and the buttocks should sit on the calf of the kneeling leg. The stepping of the left foot should be done simultaneously with the pressing of the left tiger claw. The strength should be exerted from the waist when pushing the right claw.

图 5-27　跪步推爪
Fig. 5-27 Push claw in a kneeling stance

4. 右虚步穿桥　　　　　　　Cross "bridge" in a right empty stance

右脚向前上步成右虚步；同时左虎爪变掌沿右臂下向前穿出，掌心斜向下；右虎爪变拳收至腰间，拳心向上；目视左掌。（图5-28）

要点：虚步时支撑腿脚跟不要离地；穿桥时注意左穿右拉，拧腰旋臂，腰微向右转，对称拧转。

Step forward with the right foot into a right empty stance. At the same time, change the left tiger claw into a palm and cross it forward from under the right arm, the palm facing forward. Change the right tiger claw into a fist and withdraw it to the waist, the fist center facing obliquely down. Look at the left palm. (Fig. 5-28)

Key points: Do not lift the heel of the supporting leg off the ground n the empty stance. When crossing the bridge, cross with the left palm and pull with the right one. Twist the waist and rotate the arm. Turn the waist slightly to the right side. The reverse twist action is the same.

图 5-28　右虚步穿桥
Fig. 5-28 Cross "bridge" in a right empty stance

5. 马步侧冲拳　　　　　　　　　　　Side fist thrust in a horse stance

右脚向前上步成马步，同时左掌变拳收至腰间，右拳随体转向右侧冲出，拳眼向上，臂与肩平；目视右拳。（图5-29）

要点：马步时脚跟不可离地，马步与冲拳同时完成，冲拳力达拳面，力发于腰。

Step forward with the right foot into a horse stance, and at the same time, change the left palm into a fist and draw it back to the waist. Thrust the right fist to the right side when turning right, with the fist eye facing upward. Keep arms at shoulder height. Look at the right fist. (Fig. 5-29)

Key points: Keep heels on the ground in the horse stance. Form the horse stance and thrust the fist simultaneously. Convey the thrusting strength to the fist surface. Exert strength from the waist.

图 5-29　马步侧冲拳
Fig. 5-29 Side fist thrust in a horse stance

6. 转身马步劈拳　　　Straight-arm chop with the body turning in a horse stance

身体向右后转约180°成马步；右拳变掌屈肘收至胸前，左拳由胸前随转体向左侧劈拳，臂与肩平，拳心向下；目视左拳。（图5-30）

要点：马步时脚跟不可离地，转体时重心落于右腿，劈拳动作通过转头转体带动，力达拳轮。

Turn the body to the right and move backward for about 180° to form a horse stance. Turn the right fist into a palm and bends the elbow to the chest. Move the left fist and make a straight-arm chop from the chest to the left with the turning of the body. Keep the arm at shoulder height, the fist center facing downward. Look at the left fist. (Fig. 5-30)

Key points: Keep heels on the ground in the horse stance. The center cf gravity falls on the right leg when turning the body. The straight-arm chop movement is driven by turning the head and the body. Convey the strength to "quanlun", i.e. the round hole formed on the side of the little finger.

（正面图）

图 5-30　转身马步劈拳
Fig. 5-30　Straight-arm chop with the body turning in a horse stance

（二）掌法＋拳法＋桥法＋步法＋步型
Techniques of Palm+Fist+Bridge+Step form+Step position

1.预备势 Preparatory posture

两脚并步，直腿站立，直臂两掌贴靠于两腿外侧；两掌握拳提抱于腰间，拳心向上；目视前方。（图5-31）

要点：挺胸、收腹、敛臀，提神降气。

Stand with the feet together, legs straight, arms straight, and both palms against the outside of the legs; clench both hands into fists, and then raise them around the waist, the fist centers up; look straight ahead. (Fig. 5-31)

Key points: Thrust chest forward, draw in belly, hold back buttocks, keep spirits up and lower the qi.

图 5-31 预备势
Fig. 5-31 Preparatory posture

2. 右弓步架桥　　　　　　　Build "bridge" in a right bow stance

右脚向右前方上步成半马步，两拳变掌收至左腰侧；左脚蹬地，左腿内转挺膝伸直成右弓步；同时两手臂由下向上分架于头的斜上方，掌心斜向上；目视前方。（图5-32）

要点：弓步时右膝垂直于脚背，左腿伸直；半马步转腰蓄劲，架桥时蹬地、拧腰转髋发力，臂要撑圆。

Step forward to the right side with the right foot into a half horse stance. Change both fists into palms and draw them back to the left side of the waist. Push the left leg against the ground. Turn the left leg inward and straighten the knee into a right bow stance. At the same time, place both arms diagonally above the head from bottom to top, the palms facing obliquely upward. Look straight ahead. (Fig. 5-32)

Key points: Keep the right knee perpendicular to the instep in the bow stance. Keep the left leg straight. Store up energy when turning the waist in the half horse stance. When building a "bridge", push the left leg against the ground. Exert strength when turning the waist and hips, arms forming a round circle.

图 5-32　右弓步架桥
Fig. 5-32 Build "bridge" in a right bow stance

3. 左弓步挂盖拳

Guagaiquan (Fists swing overhead)
in a left bow stance

　　左脚向前上步成左弓步，同时两掌变拳，左拳随臂外旋经上向下反挂至左后侧；右拳经上盖至体前下方，拳心斜向内；目视前方。（图5-33）

　　要点：左脚上步时微向右转腰，挂盖拳以腰带臂，幅度宜大；完成马步盖拳时，四肢对称用力，重心平稳发力于腰。

Step forward with the left foot into a left bow stance, changing both palms into fists. The left fist follows the external rotation of the arm in a top-down direction, and then hangs upside down on the left back side. Thump the right fist from the upper body to the front and lower part, the fist center facing obliquely inward. Look straight ahead. (Fig. 5-33)

Key points: When stepping forward with the left foot, turn the waist slightly to the right, and use the waist to drive arms in guagaiquan with a large range of movements. When completing gaiquan in a horse stance, exert symmetrical strength on the limbs. Be stable with the center of gravity when exerting strength from the waist.

图 5-33　左弓步挂盖拳
Fig. 5-33 Guagaiquan (Fists swing overhead) in a left bow stance

4.骑龙步撞拳　　　　　Zhuangquan (Bump fist) in a dragon-riding stance

右脚向前上步，左腿屈膝下跪成骑龙步；同时右拳随臂向上、向后经下向前上弧形撞至体前，拳心向内；左拳变掌由后向下摆至体前，附于右前臂；目视右拳。（图5-34）

要点：骑龙步时，左腿膝关节不要贴地；右拳先动，弧形抄撞，以腰带臂，上步与撞拳一致，目随右拳环视。

Step forward with the right foot, bend the left leg and kneel down into a dragon-riding stance. At the same time, the right fist follows the arm upward, backward, downward, forward and upward. Thrust it to the front of the body in an arc, with the fist center facing inward. Change the left fist into a palm, and then swing it from the back to the front of the body, attaching it to the right forearm. Look at the right fist. (Fig. 5-34)

Key points: In the dragon-riding stance, the knee of the left leg should be kept off the ground. Move the right fist first, and thrust it in an arc in the twinkling of an eye. Use the waist to drive arms. Step forward and thrust fist at the same time, and the eyes follow the right fist to look around.

图 5-34　骑龙步撞拳
Fig. 5-34 Zhuangquan (Bump fist) in a dragon-riding stance

5. 虚步切掌　　　　　　　　　　　　　Palm cutting in an empty stance

重心后移成右虚步，同时左掌沿右前臂向前横掌切出，掌指向右，掌心向下；右拳变掌随右臂内旋拉回至右胸前；目视左掌。（图5-35）

要点：右脚回收，腰微右转，右掌回拉与左掌前切用力方向相反，动作协调一致。

Move the center of gravity backward into a right empty stance, and at the same time, the left palm cuts forward horizontally along the right forearm, with the palm fingers facing right and the palm center facing down. Turn the right fist into a palm and pulls it back to the right side of the chest with the inward rotation of the right arm. Look at the left palm. (Fig. 5-35)

Key points: Withdraw the right foot. Slightly turn the waist to the right. The direction of pulling the right palm is opposite to that of the left palm cutting forward. The movements should be well coordinated.

图 5-35　虚步切掌
Fig. 5-35 Palm cutting in an empty stance

6. 马步撑掌 　　　　　　　　　　　Hold up palm in a horse stance

右脚向前上步成马步，同时右掌随体转向右侧斜下横掌切出，掌心斜向下；左掌回收至右肩前，掌心向右；目视右侧。（图5-36）

要点：马步时脚跟不可离地，马步与撑掌同时完成，切掌时右臂内旋，发力于腰。

Step forward with the right foot into a horse stance. At the same time, turn the right palm with the body turning to the right side and cuts out obliquely downward, with the palm center facing obliquely down. Draw the left palm back to the front of the right shoulder, with the palm center facing right. Look at the right palm. (Fig. 5-36)

Key points: Keep heels on the ground in the horse stance. Form the horse stance and hold up palm at the same time. The right arm rotates inward when the palm cuts. Exert strength from the waist.

图 5-36　马步撑掌
Fig. 5-36 Hold up palm in a horse stance

（三）拳法＋爪法＋步法＋跳跃＋平衡＋肘法＋步型
Techniques of Fist+Claw+Step position+Jump+Balance+Elbow+
Step form

1.预备势   Preparatory posture

两脚并步，直腿站立，直臂两掌贴靠于两腿外侧；两掌握拳提抱于腰间，拳心向上；目视前方。（图5-37）

要点：挺胸、收腹、敛臀，提神降气。

Stand with the feet together, legs straight, arms straight, and both palms against the outside of the legs; clench both hands into fists, and then raise them around the waist, the fist centers up; look straight ahead. (Fig. 5-37)

Key points: Thrust chest forward, draw in belly, hold back buttocks, keep spirits up and lower the qi.

图 5-37　预备势
Fig. 5-37 Preparatory posture

2.独立步双虎爪　　　　　　　Double tiger claw on a single foot

右脚向右前方上步，左腿屈膝提起至身前，两拳变虎爪自腰间向身体两侧推出，与肩同高；目视前方。（图5-38）

要点：独立步保持稳定，提膝要高于腰部，左脚内扣；支撑腿挺膝收髋，五趾抓地；推爪时腰先微右转。

Step forward to the right with the right foot. Bend the left leg and lift it to the front of the body, and then change fists into tiger claws, pushing them out from the waist to the sides of the body at shoulder height. Look straight ahead. (Fig. 5-38)

Key points: Keep it steady when standing on a single foot. The knee should be lifted above the waist. The left foot should be bent downward at the ankle. Keep the supporting leg and the knee straight, retracting hips and grabbing the ground with the five toes. Turn the waist slightly to the right before pushing claws.

图 5-38　独立步双虎爪
Fig. 5-38 Double tiger claw on a single foot

95

3. 左弓步双虎爪　　　　　　Double tiger claw in a left bow stance

左脚向前上步，左虎爪变拳收至左侧肩旁，拳心向右；右虎爪变拳向前方冲出，拳眼向上；右脚向前上步，右拳收至右侧肩旁，拳心向左；左拳向前冲出，拳眼向上；目视前方。

左脚蹬地向前腾空跃起，落地成半马步；同时两拳变虎爪，右虎爪收至胸前，手心向下，左虎爪盖至腹前，手心向下；右脚蹬地成左弓步，右虎爪向前平推，手心向前；左虎爪收至右肘下方，手心向下；目视前方。（图5-39）

要点：弓步时左膝垂直于脚背，右腿伸直；上步动作连贯，与上肢冲拳动作配合协调；推爪时发力于腰。

Step forward with the left foot, turn the left claw into a fist and draw it back to the side of the left shoulder, the fist center facing right. Turn the right claw into a fist and thrust it forward, the fist eye facing upward. Step forward with the right foot, draw the right fist back to the right shoulder side, the fist center facing left. Thrust the left fist forward, the fist eye facing upward. Look straight ahead.

Leap forward into the air after pushing the left foot against the ground, and land into a half-horse stance. At the same time, change both fists to tiger claws, and withdraw the right one to the front of the chest, the claw center facing downward. Cover the left claw to the front of the abdomen, the claw center facing downward. Form a left bow stance after pushing the right foot against the ground. Push the right claw forward, with the claw center facing forward. Withdraw the left claw under the right elbow, the claw center facing downward. Look straight ahead. (Fig. 5-39)

Key points: Keep the left knee perpendicular to the instep in the bow stance, the right leg straight. Step up smoothly, and coordinate it well with fist thrusts. Exert strength from the waist when pushing claws.

图 5-39　左弓步双虎爪
Fig. 5-39 Double tiger claw in a left bow stance

4. 左骑龙步压肘　　　　　　　　　Press elbow in a left dragon-riding stance

左脚向后撤步，左爪变掌自右臂下方向左前穿出，右爪变拳收至右肩侧；右脚向后撤步成左骑龙步，同时右肘尖向左斜下方压肘，左掌覆于右手肘部；目视右肘。（图5-40）

要点：压肘时腰微右转，骑龙步与压肘动作一致，力达肘部。

Step back with the left foot, and change the left claw into a palm before thrusting it forward from under the right arm to the left front. Change the right claw into a fist and draw it back to the side of the right shoulder. Step backward with the right foot into a left dragon-riding stance, while pressing the elbow diagonally downward with the tip of the right elbow, the left palm resting on the right elbow. Look at the right elbow. (Fig. 5-40)

Key points: When pressing the elbow, turn the waist slightly to the right. The dragon riding stance is formed simultaneously with the pressing of the elbow. Convey the strength to the elbow.

图 5-40　左骑龙步压肘
Fig. 5-40 Press elbow in a left dragon-riding stance

5. 右骑龙步冲拳　　　　　　　　Thrust fist in a right dragon-riding stance

身体右转，成右骑龙步；同时右拳向后收至右侧肩侧，左掌变拳向前冲出，拳眼向上；目视前方。（图5-41）

要点：骑龙步时左腿膝关节不要贴地；骑龙步与冲拳动作一致，冲拳时力达拳面。

Turn the body to the right into a right dragon-riding stance, and at the same time, withdraw the right fist back to the side of the right shoulder, change the left palm into a fist and thrust it forward, with the fist eye facing upward. Look straight ahead. (Fig. 5-41)

Key points: In the dragon-riding stance, the knee of the left leg should be kept off the ground. The dragon-riding stance is formed simultaneously with fist thrust. Convey the strength to the surface of the fist.

图 5-41　右骑龙步冲拳
Fig. 5-41 Thrust fist in a right dragon-riding stance

6. 左弓步抛拳　　　　　　　　　　Throw fist in a left bow stance

左脚向左前活步成左弓步，同时右拳由右侧随转体向右上抛起，拳眼向右，左拳经下挂摆至左后侧举，拳心向下；目视前方。（图5-42）

要点：抛拳时步幅移动不宜太大，上肢动作幅度宜大，注意以腰带臂。

Step forward with the left foot to the left side and form a left bow stance. At the same time, throw the right fist up from the right to the right upper side with the turning of the body, the fist eye facing right. Swing the left fist from below to the left back side with a side lift, the fist eye facing downward. Look straight ahead. (Fig. 5-42)

Key points: When throwing fist, do not make a big stride. Use the waist to drive arms with a large range of movements of the upper body.

图 5-42　左弓步抛拳
Fig. 5-42 Throw fist in a left bow stance

南拳段前五级   Nan Quan: Pre-Duan Level 5

南拳段前五级
Nan Quan: Pre-
Duan Level 5

（一）拳法＋掌法＋爪法＋桥法＋步法＋步型
Techniques of Fist+Palm+Claw+Bridge+Step position+Step form

1. 预备势   Preparatory posture

两脚并步，直腿站立，直臂两掌贴靠于两腿外侧；两掌握拳提抱于腰间，拳心向上；目视前方。（图5-43）

要点：挺胸、收腹、敛臀，提神降气。

Stand with the feet together, legs straight, arms straight, and both palms against the outside of the legs; clench both hands into fists, and then raise them around the waist, the fist centers up; look straight ahead. (Fig. 5-43)

Key points: Thrust chest forward, draw in belly, hold back buttocks, keep spirits up and lower the qi.

图 5-43 预备势
Fig. 5-43 Preparatory posture

2. 半马步截桥　　　　　　　Jieqiao (Cut "bridge") in a half horse stance

右脚向右移动成半马步；右拳向右侧截劈，拳心向下，左掌收至右肩旁，掌心向外；目视右拳。（图5-44）

要点：移步与转体、截桥一致，右臂的运行幅度宜小，力达前臂尺骨侧（小指一侧）。

Step to the right with the right foot and form a half horse stance, the right fist cutting to the right, the fist center facing down. Draw the left palm to the side of the right shoulder, the palm facing outward. Look at the right fist. (Fig. 5-44)

Key points: Move the foot, turn the body and cut the bridge at the same time. Move the right arm with a small range. Convey the strength to the ulnar side of forearm (the side of the little finger).

图 5-44　半马步截桥
Fig. 5-44 Jieqiao (Cut "bridge") in a half horse stance

3. 右弓步滚桥   Gunqiao ("Bridge" rolling) in a right bow stance

左脚蹬地，左腿内转挺膝伸直成右弓步；同时左拳向右前方滚桥，拳眼斜向下，右拳变掌收于左肩，掌指斜向上；目视前方。（图5-45）

要点：弓步时右膝垂直于脚背；左腿蹬转，扣膝、转胯、转腰发力，发力时上下肢协调一致，滚桥力达前臂。

Push the left foot against the ground, turn the left leg inward and straighten the knee to form a right bow stance. At the same time, the left fist rolls forward to the right, the fist eye facing obliquely downward. Change the right fist into a palm and draw it back to the left shoulder, with the palm fingers facing upward. Look straight ahead. (Fig. 5-45)

Key points: When forming the bow stance, the right knee is perpendicular to the instep. Push and turn the left leg, twist the knee, turn the hips, and turn the waist to exert strength. When exerting strenth, the upper and lower limbs are well coordinated. Convey the strength to the forearm when rolling the bridge.

图 5-45　右弓步滚桥
Fig. 5-45 Gunqiao ("bridge" rolling) in a right bow stance

4. 左右弓步抛拳　　　　　　Throw fist in a left and right bow stance

左脚向前上步成左弓步；左拳经下挂摆至左后侧举，拳心向下；右掌变拳由右侧随转体向右上抛起，拳眼向后；目视前方。右脚向前上步成右弓步，左拳由左侧随转体向左上抛起，拳眼向后；右拳经下挂摆至右后侧举，拳心向下；目视前方。（图5-46）

要点：左右抛拳步幅移动不宜太大，稍作活步即可；上肢动作幅度宜大，注重以腰带臂，左右拧转对称用力。

Step forward with the left foot to form a left bow stance. Swing the left fist from the bottom and raise it to the left back side, with the fist center facing down. Turn the right palm into a fist, and throw it up from the right side with the body turning, the fist eye facing to the right. Look straight ahead. Step forward with the right foot to form a right bow stance. Throw the left fist up from the left with the body turning, the fist eye facing to the left. Swing the right from below to the right back side with a side lift, the fist eye facing downward. Look straight ahead. (Fig. 5-46)

Key points: When throwing the fist left and right fist in a bow stance, do not make a big stride. Just have a moving step. Use the waist to drive arms with a large range of movements of the upper body. Exert symmetrical strength when twisting left and right.

图 5-46　左右弓步抛拳
Fig. 5-46 Throw fist in a left and right bow stance

5. 左弓步抓面爪　　　　　　　　　Scratch-face claw in a left bow stance

左脚向左侧上步成半马步，同时两拳变虎爪，右虎爪收于胸前，手心斜向下，左虎爪由上扣按至左侧，手心斜向下；右腿内转挺膝伸直成左弓步，右虎爪由腰间向前直抓，手心向前，左虎爪收至右肘内侧下方，手心向右；目视前方。（图5-47）

要点：半马步闭气蓄劲，腰微右转，意在左虎爪的扣按（防守之意），右虎爪前抓时注重右腿的蹬转，力起于根。

Step forward with the left foot to the left side to form a half horse stance. At the same time, change both fists into tiger claws. Draw the right tiger claw back to the chest, the claw center facing obliquely downward. Press the left tiger claw from the top to the left side, the claw center facing obliquely downward. Turn the right leg inward and straighten the knee to form a left bow stance. The right tiger claw scratches straight ahead from the waist, with the claw center facing forward. Withdraw the left tiger claw under the inner side of the right elbow, with the claw center facing right. Look straight ahead. (Fig. 5-47)

Key points: Hold breath to store up energy in the half horse stance, and turn the waist slightly to the right in order to press the left tiger claw (for defense). Push and turn the right leg when the right claw scratches, with the strength from the root, i.e. feet.

图 5-47　左弓步抓面爪
Fig. 5-47　Scratch-face claw in a left bow stance

6. 虚步冲拳推掌 Thrust fist and push palm in an empty stance

右脚向右前上半步，右虎爪变拳收至右胸前，左虎爪变掌摆按至右胸前；左脚向左前上步成左虚步，右拳、左掌随转体向正前方冲拳、推掌，两臂与肩同高、同宽，右拳心向下，左掌指向上；目视前方。（图5-48）

要点：步法移动时重心下沉，虚步重心在右腿，虚实分明 冲拳、推掌发力于腰，眼随手动。

Make a half step forward to the right with the right foot. Turn the right tiger claw into a fist and draw it back to the waist. Turn the left tiger claw into a palm, swing and press it to the right side of the chest. Step forward to the left with left foot and form a left empty stance. Thrust the right fist and push the left palm straight ahead with the body turning, both arms at shoulder height and shoulder-width apart, with the right fist center facing down and the fingers of the left palm facing up. Look straight ahead. (Fig. 5-48)

Key points: When changing the step position, move the center of gravity downward. The weight is on the right leg in an empty stance. Differentiate between "Xu" and "Shi" (Make clear of empty and solid movements). Exert strength from the waist when thrusting fist and pushing palm, eyes following the movement of hands.

图 5-48 虚步冲拳推掌
Fig. 5-48 Thrust fist and push palm in an empty stance

（二）拳法＋爪法＋腿法＋步法＋步型
Techniques of Fist+Claw+Leg+Step form+Step position

1.预备势   Preparatory posture

两脚并步，直腿站立，直臂两掌贴靠于两腿外侧；两掌握拳提抱于腰间，拳心向上；目视前方。（图5-49）

要点：挺胸、收腹、敛臀，提神降气。

Stand with the feet together, legs straight, arms straight, and both palms against the outside of the legs; clench both hands into fists, and then raise them around the waist, the fist centers up; look straight ahead. (Fig. 5-49)

Key points: Thrust chest forward, draw in belly, hold back buttocks, keep spirits up and lower the qi.

图 5-49 预备势
Fig. 5-49 Preparatory posture

2. 骑龙步冲拳　　　　　　　　　Thrust fist in a dragon-rid ng stance

左脚向前上步，右腿屈膝下跪成骑龙步；同时右手冲拳，拳眼向上；左拳变掌架至左侧头顶上方，掌心向上；目视右拳。（图5-50）

要点：骑龙步时右腿膝关节不要贴地；上步与冲拳一致，冲拳时腰微右转，力达拳面，发力于腰。

Step forward with the left foot, bend the right leg and kneel down irto a dragon-riding stance. At the same time, thrust the right fist with the fist eye facing up. Change the left fist into a palm and place it on the top left side of the head, with the palm facing upward. Look at the right fist. (Fig. 5-50)

Key points: The knee joint of the right leg should not touch the ground when forming the dragon-riding stance. Step forward and thrust fist at the same time. Turn the waist slightly to the right when thrusting fist. Convey the strength to the fist surface. Exert strength from the waist.

图 5-50　骑龙步冲拳
Fig. 5-50 Thrust fist in a dragon-riding stance

3. 高虚步鞭拳　　　　　　　　　Whip fist in a high empty stance

左脚向前活步，左掌变拳向左前方鞭拳，右拳变掌摆至左肩侧；右脚向前上步成高虚步，同时右掌变拳向右前方鞭拳，左拳变掌摆至右肩侧，掌心向右；目视右拳。（图5-51）

要点：移动步幅要小，上步与鞭拳一致，冲拳时发力于腰，力达拳背。

Make a moving step forward with the left foot. Change the left palm into a fist which whips to the front left. Turn he right fist into a palm and swing it to the left shoulder side. Step forward with the right foot to form a high empty stance. At the same time, change the right palm into a fist and whip forward to the right. Turn the left fist into a palm and swing it to the right shoulder side, the fist center facing to the right. Look at the right fist. (Fig. 5-51)

Key points: Move the foot with a small range. Step forward and whip fist at the same time. Exert strength from the waist when thrusting fist, and convey the strength to the fist back.

图 5-51　高虚步鞭拳
Fig. 5-51 Whip fist in a high empty stance

4. 左弓步冲拳　　　　　　　　　　　Thrust fist in a left bow stance

右脚向右后方撤步成左弓步，同时右拳直线向前冲出，拳心向下；左掌变拳收抱于腰间，拳心向上；目视前方。（图5-52）

要点：弓步时左膝垂直于脚背，右腿伸直，右脚全脚掌贴地；右脚撤步的同时要转腰；冲拳时力发于腰，力达拳面，劲力完整。

Step back to the right with the right foot to form a left bow stance, and at the same time thrust the right fist straight ahead, with the fist center facing down. Withdraw the left fist to the waist, with the fist cente facing upward. Look straight ahead. (Fig. 5-52)

Key points: Keep the left knee perpendicular to the instep in the bow stance, the right leg straight and the whole right foot on the ground. Step back with the right foot while turning the waist. Exert full strength from the waist when thrusting fist, and convey the strength to the fist surface.

图 5-52　左弓步冲拳
Fig. 5-52 Thrust fist in a left bow stance

5. 横钉腿右弓步侧冲拳 — Side fist thrusting and sideways leg nailing in a right bow stance

左脚不动，右腿从侧方向前由屈到伸横向钉击；同时右拳收至腰间，左拳变掌，向前切掌，掌尖向右；目视前方。右脚下落，同时左掌变拳收至腰间，右拳向前冲拳，拳眼向上；左腿蹬转成右弓步，右拳收至腰间，左拳向前冲拳，拳眼向上；目视前方。（图5-53）

要点：横钉腿钉出时后膝关节挺直，右脚尖勾起，力达前脚掌；冲拳时力起于根（左脚），上下肢协调用力。

Keep the left foot still. Extend the right leg from its bending position, and then make a nailing strike from the side to the front. At the same time, withdraw the right fist to the waist, changing the left fist into a palm and cutting it forward, the palm tip facing to the right. Look straight ahead. Put down the right foot while changing the left palm into a fist and drawing it back to the waist. Thrust the right fist forward, the fist eye facing upward. Push the left leg against ground and turn the body to form a right bow stance, withdraw the right fist to the waist, and thrust the left fist forward, the fist eye facing upward. Look straight ahead. (Fig. 5-53)

Key points: Keep the knee joint straight after the sideways nailing strike, raise the toes of the right foot, and convey the strength to the forefoot. When thrusting fist, the strength is from the root (the left foot). Keep a good coordination of upper and lower limbs when exerting strength.

图 5-53　横钉腿右弓步侧冲拳
Fig. 5-53 Side fist thrusting and sideways leg nailing in a right bow stance

（三）拳法＋肘法＋步法＋格打＋桥法＋步法＋步型
Techniques of Fist+Elbow+Step position+Grappling+Bridge+
Step position+Step form

1. 预备势　　　　　　　　　　　　　　　　Preparatory posture

两脚并步，直腿站立，直臂两掌贴靠于两腿外侧；两掌握拳提抱于腰间，拳心向上；目视前方。（图5-54）

要点：挺胸、收腹、敛臀，提神降气。

Stand with the feet together, legs straight, arms straight, and both palms against the outside of the legs; clench both hands into fists, and then raise them around the waist, the fist centers up; look straight ahead. (Fig. 5-54)

Key points: Thrust chest forward, draw in belly, hold back buttocks, keep spirits up and lower the qi.

图 5-54　预备势
Fig. 5-54 Preparatory posture

2. 半马步侧冲拳   Side fist thrust in a half horse stance

右脚向右前方上步，成半马步；同时右拳随转体向前冲拳，拳眼向上，左拳变掌收至右胸前，掌心向右；目视右拳。（图5-55）

要点：半马步冲拳时要与转体一致，发力于腰，力达拳面。

Step forward to the right with the right foot into a half horse stance, and at the same time, thrust the right fist forward while turning the body, with the fist eye facing upward. Change the left fist into a palm and withdraw it to the front of the right side of the chest, with the palm facing right. Look at the right fist. (Fig. 5-55)

Key points: Thrust the fist in a half horse stance while turning the body. Exert strength from the waist and convey it to the fist surface.

图 5-55　半马步侧冲拳
Fig. 5-55 Side fist thrust in a half horse stance

3. 左弓步挂盖拳   Guagaiquan (Fists swing overhead) in a left bow stance

左脚向前上步，成左弓步。同时左掌变拳随臂外旋经上向下反挂至左后侧，右拳经上盖至体前下方，拳心斜向内；目视前方。（图5-56）

要点：左脚上步时腰微向右转；挂盖拳以腰带臂，幅度宜大；完成弓步盖拳时，四肢对称用力，重心平稳，发力于腰。

Step forward with the left foot into a left bow stance, changing the left palm into a fist before it follows the external rotation of the arm in a top-down direction, and then hangs upside down on the left back side. Thump the right fist from the upper body to the front and lower part, the fist center facing obliquely inward. Look straight ahead. (Fig. 5-56)

Key points: When stepping forward with the left foot, turn the waist slightly to the right, and use the waist to drive arms in guagaiquan with a large range of movements. When completing gaiquan in a horse stance, exert symmetrical strength on the limbs. Be stable with the center of gravity when exerting strength from the waist.

图 5-56　左弓步挂盖拳
Fig. 5-56 Guagaiquan (Fists swing overhead) in a left bow stance

4. 退步格打   Step back to grapple

左脚向后撤步，同时右拳以肘关节为轴由内经上向外收至右腰侧，左拳屈肘由后经下向里挂挑至左肩前，拳心向内；右脚向后撤步成左弓步，左拳收至腰间，右拳向前平冲，拳心向下；目视前方。（图5-57）

要点：左脚退步时完成右、左拳的挂挑，右腿落步与冲拳一致，冲拳时腰微左转，力达拳面。

Step back with the left foot, and at the same time, using the elbow joint as the axis, withdraw the right fist to the right side of the waist in an inside-upside-outside direction. Bend the left elbow, and lift the left fist to the front of the left shoulder in a backside-downside-inside direction, the fist center facing inward. Step back with the right foot into a left bow stance, withdraw the left fist to the waist, and thrust the right fise straight forward, with the fist center facing downward. Look straight ahead. (Fig. 5-57)

Key points: When stepping back with the left foot, complete the hanging and lifting of the right and left fist. The stepping of the right leg and fist thrusting are completed at the same time. Turn the waist slightly to the left when thrusting, and convey the strength to the fist surface.

图 5-57　退步格打
Fig. 5-57 Step back to grapple

5. 插步撞肘   Bump elbow with a back cross-step

左脚向后插步，同时右臂向后顶肘，与肩同高，左拳变掌，附于右拳拳面，掌指向上；目视右肘。（图5-58）

要点：插步与顶肘要一致，腰微右转，力达肘尖。

Step back with the left foot, and form a cross-step position. At the same time, push the elbow backward with the right hand at shoulder height. Change the left fist into a palm, and attach it to the right fist surface, with the palm fingers pointing upward. Look at the right elbow. (Fig. 5-58)

Key points: Complete the back cross-step and elbow pushing at the same time. Turn the waist slightly to the right. Convey the strength to the tip of the elbow.

图 5-58　插步撞肘
Fig. 5-58 Bump elbow with a back cross-step

6. 左弓步劈桥　　　　　　　　　Chop "bridge" in a left bow stance

右脚向后撤步，成左弓步；同时右臂以尺骨侧为力点，由下向上经头顶下劈，左掌变拳抱于腰间，拳心向上；目视右拳。（图5-59）

要点：右拳上举时，目随右拳环视；劈桥时右臂外旋，力达前臂，屈肘下沉。

Step back with the right foot to form a left bow stance. At the same time, move the right arm from bottom to top, and chop it down from above the head by exerting strength from the ulnar side. Hold the left fist to the waist, with the fist center facing upward. Look at the right fist. (Fig. 5-59)

Key points: When the right fist is lifted, the eyes follow the right fist to look around. When chopping the bridge, the right arm is rotated externally. The strength reaches the forearm. Lower the elbow and bend it.

图 5-59　左弓步劈桥
Fig. 5-59 Chop "bridge" in a left bow stance

南拳段前六级　　　　　Nan Quan: Pre-Duan Level 6

南拳段前六级
Nan Quan: Pre-
Duan Level 6

（一）拳法＋掌法＋爪法＋步法＋步型
Techniques of Fist+Palm+Claw+Step position+Step form

1.预备势　　　　　　　　　　　　　　　Preparatory posture

两脚并步，直腿站立，直臂两掌贴靠于两腿外侧；两掌握拳提抱于腰间，拳心向上；目视前方。（图5-60）

要点：挺胸、收腹、敛臀，提神降气。

Stand with the feet together, legs straight, arms straight, and both palms against the outside of the legs; clench both hands into fists, and then raise them around the waist, the fist centers up; look straight ahead. (Fig. 5-60)

Key points: Thrust chest forward, draw in belly, hold back buttocks, keep spirits up and lower the qi.

图 5-60　预备势
Fig. 5-60 Preparatory posture

117

2. 马步双标掌   Thrust palms in a horse stance

左脚向左开步，成马步；同时两拳变掌直线向前标出，两臂与肩同高、同宽，掌心向下；目视前方。（图5-61）

要点：马步时脚跟不可离地，标掌时腰先微右转，以腰发力。

Step to the left with the left foot and form a horse stance. At the same time, turn fists into palms and thrust them straight forward, with both arms at shoulder height and shoulder-width apart, both palms facing downward. Look straight ahead. (Fig. 5-61)

Key points: Keep heels on the ground in the horse stance. Turn the waist slightly to the right when thrusting palms. Exert strength from the waist.

图 5-61　马步双标掌
Fig. 5-61 Thrust palms in a horse stance

3. 右弓步蝶掌　　　　　　　Butterfly palm in a right bow stance

右脚向前成右弓步，左腿伸直，左脚全脚掌贴地；两掌向前推出，右掌在上，掌指向上，左掌在下，掌指向下，两掌相距20～30厘米；目视前方。（图5-62）

要点：弓步时右膝垂直于脚背，推掌时要蹬脚、扣膝、拧腰转髋发力，发力时上下肢协调一致。

Step forward with the right foot into a right bow stance, keeping the left leg straight, and the sole of the left foot on the ground. Push both palms forward, with the right palm on the top and the palm fingers facing up; the left palm on the bottom and the palm fingers facing down. Keep the distance between the two palms 20-30 cm. Look straight ahead. (Fig. 5-62)

Key points: Keep the right knee perpendicular to the instep in the bow stance. When pushing the palms, kick with heel, twist the knees, turn the waist and hips to exert force. The upper and lower limbs should be well coordinated in strength exertion.

图 5-62　右弓步蝶掌
Fig. 5-62 Butterfly palm in a right bow stance

4. 左右弓步抛拳   Throw fist in a left and right bow stance

左脚向前上步，右腿向前跟进成左弓步；同时左掌变拳经下挂摆至左后侧平举，拳心向下；右拳由右侧随转体向右上抛起，拳眼向后。右脚向前上步，左腿向前跟进成右弓步；同时右拳经下挂摆至右后侧平举，拳心向下；左拳由左侧随转体向左上抛起，拳眼向左；目视前方。（图5-63）

要点：左右抛拳步幅移动不宜太大，稍作活步即可；上肢动作幅度宜大，注意以腰带臂，左右拧转对称用力。

Step forward with the left foot, and the right leg follows up to form a left bow stance. At the same time, change the left palm into a fist, swing it from the bottom to the left back side, and hold flat, with the fist center facing down. Throw the right fist up from the right side with the turning of the body, the fist eye facing right. Step forward with the right foot, and the left leg follows up to form a right bow stance. At the same time, swing the right fist from the bottom to the right back side, and hold flat, with the fist center facing down. Throw the left fist up from the left side with the turning of the body, the fist eye facing left. Look straight ahead. (Fig. 5-63)

Key points: When throwing the fist in a left and right bow stance, do not make a big stride. Just have a moving step. Use the waist to drive arms with a large range cf movements of the upper body. Exert symmetrical strength when twisting left and right.

图 5-63　左右弓步抛拳
Fig. 5-63 Throw fist in a left and right bow stance

5. 左弓步挂盖拳

Guagaiquan (Fists swing overhead) in a left bow stance

左脚向前上步，成左弓步；同时腰微右转，左拳随臂内旋由上向下经体前反挂至左后侧，右拳经上盖至体前下方，拳心斜向内；目视前方。（图5-64）

要点：左脚上步时，微向右转腰；挂盖拳以腰带臂，幅度宜大；完成弓步盖拳时，四肢对称用力，重心平稳，发力于腰。

Step forward with the left foot into a left bow stance while turning the waist slightly to the right. The left fist follows the internal rotation of the arm in a top-down direction, and then hangs upside down on the left back side. Thump the right fist from the upper body to the front and lower part of the body, the fist center facing obliquely inward. Look straight ahead. (Fig. 5-64)

Key points: When stepping forward with the left foot, turn the waist slightly to the right, and use the waist to drive arms in guagaiquan with a large range of movements. When completing gaiquan in a horse stance, exert symmetrical strength on the limbs. Be stable with the center of gravity while exerting strength from the waist.

图 5-64　左弓步挂盖拳
Fig. 5-64 Guagaiquan (Fists swing overhead) in a left bow stance

6. 骑龙步撞拳　　　Zhuangquan (Bump fist) in a dragon-riding stance

右脚向前上步，左腿屈膝下跪成骑龙步；同时右拳随臂向上、向后经下向前上弧形撞至体前，拳心向内，左拳变掌由后向下摆至体前，附于右前臂；目视右拳。（图5-65）

要点：骑龙步时，左腿膝关节不要贴地；右拳先动，弧形抄撞，以腰带臂；上步与撞拳一致，目随右拳环视。

Step forward with the right foot, bend the left knee and kneel down into a dragon-riding stance. At the same time, bump the right fist to the front of the body after it moves in an arc shape by following the arm upward, backward, downward, forward and upward. with the fist center facing inward. Change the left fist into a palm, and then swing it from the back to the front of the body, attaching it to the right forearm. Look at the right fist. (Fig. 5-65)

Key points: In the dragon-riding stance, the knee of the left leg should be kept off the ground. Move the right fist first, and bump it in an arc in the twinkling of an eye. Use the waist to drive arms. Stepping forward and fist thrusting are completed at the same time, and the eyes follow the right fist to look around.

图 5-65　骑龙步撞拳
Fig. 5-65 Zhuangquan (Bump fist) in a dragon-riding stance

（二）拳法 + 平衡 + 桥法 + 步型 + 步法
Techniques of Fist+Balance+Bridge+Step form+Step position

1. 预备势   Preparatory posture

两脚并步，直腿站立，直臂两掌贴靠于两腿外侧；两掌握拳提抱于腰间，拳心向上；目视前方。（图5-66）

要点：挺胸、收腹、敛臀，提神降气。

Stand with the feet together, legs straight, arms straight, and both palms against the outside of the legs; clench both hands into fists, and then raise them around the waist, the fist center sup; look straight ahead. (Fig. 5-66)

Key points: Thrust chest forward, draw in belly, hold back buttocks, keep spirits up and lower the qi.

图 5-66　预备势
Fig. 5-66 Preparatory posture

2. 独立步截桥
Jieqiao (Cut "bridge") on a single foot

左脚向前上步，右腿屈膝提起成独立步；同时右拳向右后侧截劈，拳心向下，左拳变掌摆至右胸前，掌心向右；目视右拳。（图5-67）

要点：独立步提膝要高于腰部，右脚须内扣；截桥时上下肢动作一致，身体微右转，以腰带臂，力达前臂尺骨侧（小指一侧）。

Step forward with the left foot, bend the right knee and lift the right leg to stand on a single foot; at the same time, the right fist cuts to the right back side, the fist center facing down. Turn the left fist into a palm and swing it to the front of the right side of the chest, the palm facing to the right. Look at the right fist. (Fig. 5-67)

Key points: When forming the single-foot position, the knee should be raised above the waist, and the right foot should be bent downward at the ankle. When cutting the bridge, the upper and lower limbs move in the same way. Turn the body slightly to the right, and use the waist to drive arms. Convey the strength to the ulnar side of forearm (the side of the little finger).

图 5-67 独立步截桥
Fig. 5-67 Jieqiao (Cut "bridge") on a single foot

3. 弓步挂盖拳   Guagaiquan (Fists swing overhead) in a bow stance

右脚落地后，左脚向前上步成左弓步；左掌变拳随臂外旋经上向下反挂至左后侧；右拳经上盖至体前下方，拳心斜向内；目视前方。（图5-68）

要点：左脚上步时微向右转腰；挂盖拳以腰带臂，幅度宜大；完成弓步盖拳时，四肢对称用力，重心平稳，发力于腰。

After landing the right foot, step forward with the left foot to form a left bow stance, the left fist follows the external rotation of the arm in a top-down direction, and then hangs upside down on the left back side. Thump the right fist from the upper body to the front and lower part of the body, the fist center facing obliguely inward. Look straight ahead. (Fig. 5-68)

Key points: When stepping forward with the left foot, turn the waist slightly to the right, and use the waist to drive arms in guagaiquan with a large range of movements. When completing gaiquan in a horse stance, exert symmetrical strength on the limbs. Be stable with the center of gravity while exerting strength from the waist.

图 5-68　弓步挂盖拳
Fig. 5-68 Guagaiquan (Fists swing overhead) in a bow stance

4. 插步鞭拳   Whip fist in a back cross-step

右脚向前上步，脚尖斜向左，左脚插步落于右腿后方；同时右拳向插步方向鞭击，拳眼向上；左拳变掌经胸前摆至右肩前，掌指向上；目视右拳。（图5-69）

要点：插步与鞭拳动作要一致，鞭拳时力达拳背。

Step forward with the right foot, toes pointing to obliquely left, and make a back cross-step with the left foot landing behind the right leg; at the same time, whip the right fist in the direction of the back cross-step, with the fist eye facing upward. Change the left fist into a palm and swing it through the chest to the front of the right shoulder, with the palm fingers facing upward. Look at the right fist. (Fig. 5-69)

Key points: Form the back cross-step and whip the fist at the same time. Convey the strength to the fist back when whipping.

图 5-69　插步鞭拳
Fig. 5-69 Whip fist in a back cross-step

5. 转身挂盖拳　　　　Guagaiquan (Fists swing overhead) with body turning

身体左转，左脚向前上步成左弓步；同时左掌变拳随臂外旋经上向下反挂至左后侧，右拳经上盖至体前下方，拳心斜向内；目视前方。（图5-70）

要点：挂盖拳以腰带臂，幅度宜大，完成弓步盖拳时，四肢对称用力，重心平稳，发力于腰。

Turn the body to the left, and step forward with the left foot to form a left bow stance; at the same time, the left fist follows the external rotation of the arm in a top-down direction, and then hangs upside down on the left back side. Thump the right fist from the upper body to the front and lower part of the body, the fist center facing obliquely inward. Look straight ahead. (Fig. 5-70)

Key points: Use the waist to drive arms in guagaiquan with a large range of movements. When completing gaiquan in a horse stance, exert symmetrical strength on the limbs. Be stable with the center of gravity when exerting strength from the waist.

图 5-70　转身挂盖拳
Fig. 5-70 Guagaiquan (Fists swing overhead) with body turning

6. 马步侧冲拳   Side fist thrust in a horse stance

右脚向前上步成马步，两拳变掌，两臂向上、向后经下向前弧形收至腰间；右掌变拳随身体转动向前冲拳，拳眼向上；左拳变掌屈肘收至右胸前，掌心向右；目视右拳。（图5-71）

要点：马步时脚跟不可离地；马步冲拳时要与转体一致，发力于腰，力达拳面。

Step forward with the right leg into a horse stance, changing fists into palms. Move the arms in an up-back-down-forward direction like an arc and place them to the waist. Change the right palm into a fist and thrust it forward with the turning of the body, the fist eye facing upward. Bend the left elbow and withdraw the left palm to the front of the right side of the chest, the palm facing to the right. Look at the right fist. (Fig. 5-71)

Key points: Keep heels on the ground in the horse stance. Form the stance and thrust fist simultaneously. Exert strength from the waist, and convey it to the fist surface.

图 5-71　马步侧冲拳
Fig. 5-71 Side fist thrust in a horse stance

（三）拳法＋肘法＋桥法＋腿法＋步法＋指法＋步型
Techniques of Fist+Elbow+Bridge+Leg+Step position+
Finger+Step form

1.预备势   Preparatory posture

两脚并步，直腿站立，直臂两掌贴靠于两腿外侧；两掌握拳提抱于腰间，拳心向上；目视前方。（图5-72）

要点：挺胸、收腹、敛臀，提神降气。

Stand with the feet together, legs straight, arms straight, and both palms against the outside of the legs; clench both hands into fists, and then raise them around the waist, the fist centers up; look straight ahead. (Fig. 5-72)

Key points: Thrust chest forward, draw in belly, hold back buttocks, keep spirits up and lower the qi.

图 5-72　预备势
Fig. 5-72 Preparatory posture

2.上步单拍脚   Step up to slap one foot

左脚向前上步，右腿直摆向上，脚面绷起；右拳变掌，拍击右脚脚面，拍击位置与肩同高；目视右掌。（图5-73）

要点：拍脚时身体直立，两腿挺直，击响干脆。

Step up forward with the left foot, swing the right leg straight up, and stretch the foot. Turn the right fist into a palm, and slap the right foot at shoulder height. Look at the right palm. (Fig. 5-73)

Key points: When slapping the feet, keep the body upright and the legs straight. Make a clear-cut slap.

图 5-73　上步单拍脚
Fig. 5-73 Step up to slap one foot

3. 半马步侧冲拳　　　　　　Side fist thrust in a half horse stance

右脚向右前方落地成半马步；同时右掌变拳随转体向前冲拳，左拳收至左侧腰间，拳心向上；目视右拳。（图5-74）

要点：半马步冲拳时要与转体一致，发力于腰，力达拳面。

Step forward to the right with the right foot into a half horse stance, and at the same time, thrust the right fist forward while turning the body, and withdraw the left fist to the left side of the waist, the fist eye facing upward. Look at the right fist. (Fig. 5-74)

Key points: Thrust the fist in a half horse stance while turning the body. Exert strength from the waist and convey it to the fist surface.

图 5-74　半马步侧冲拳
Fig. 5-74 Side fist thrust in a half horse stance

4. 单蝶步压肘   Press elbow in a single fold stance

身体直立，左拳变掌沿右臂下方向前穿出，右拳收至右侧肩旁；左脚向前上步蹬地跃起，身体直立在空中旋转360°，落地后左腿屈膝全蹲成单蝶步；同时右臂向下压肘，左掌附于右臂肘部，目视前方。（图5-75）

要点：单蝶步时右腿小腿及脚踝内侧要贴地，空中转体保持身体直立，单蝶步与压肘一致，压肘时腰微左转。

Keep the body upright. Change the left fist into a palm which passes forward from under the right arm, and draw back the right fist to the right shoulder side. Step up forward with the left foot and jumps off the ground, keeping the body upright in the air and rotating it for 360°. After landing, the left leg is fully bent to form a single fold stance; at the same time, the right arm presses down on the elbow, the left palm attached to the right elbow. Look straight ahead. (Fig. 5-75)

Key points: Make the inner side of the calf and ankle close to the ground in a single fold stance. When turning the body in the air, keep it upright. Form the single fold stance and press the elbow at the same time. Turn the waist slightly to the left when pressing the elbow.

图 5-75　单蝶步压肘
Fig. 5-75 Press elbow in a single fold stance

5. 骑龙步劈桥   Chop "bridge" in a dragon-riding stance

原地身体直立，右拳由下向上举至头顶上方，左掌下按至体侧；左腿屈膝半蹲成骑龙步，同时右臂外旋向体前下劈，左掌摆至右上臂内侧，掌心向右；目视右拳方向。（图5-76）

要点：右拳上举时，注意手眼配合；劈桥时右臂外旋，屈肘下沉。

Stand upright on the spot, raise the right fist up above the head from bottom, and press the left palm down to the front of the body. Bend the left knee and do a half squat to form a dragon-riding stance; at the same time, the right arm rotates outward and chops down in front of the body. Swing the left palm to the inside of the right upper arm, the palm facing to the right. Look at the right fist. (Fig. 5-76)

Key points: Have a good hand-eye coordination when raising up the right fist. When chopping the "bridge", swing the right arm outward and lower the right elbow.

图 5-76 骑龙步劈桥
Fig. 5-76 Chop "bridge" in a dragon-riding stance

6. 右弓步侧推指　　　　　　　Side finger push in a right bow stance

　　右脚活步成右弓步；同时左掌变单指手向前推出，臂与肩平；右拳收至右侧腰间；目视左指尖。（图5-77）

　　要点：弓步时右膝垂直于脚背；单指手前推时注意左腿的蹬转，力发于根，完整发力。

Move the right foot and form a right bow stance. At the same time, change the left palm into the single-finger position and push it forward, arms at shoulder height. Withdraw the right fist to the right side of the waist. Look at the left fingertip. (Fig. 5-77)

Key points: When forming the bow stance, the right knee is perpendicular to the instep. Push and turn the left leg when pushing the finger. Exert full strength from the root.

图 5-77　右弓步侧推指
Fig. 5-77 Side finger push in a right bow stance

南拳段前七级　　　　　　　　Nan Quan: Pre-Duan Level 7

南拳段前七级
Nan Quan: Pre-
Duan Level 7

（一）拳法＋桥法＋掌法＋步法＋步型
Techniques of Fist+Bridge+Palm+Step position+Step form

1. 左弓步侧冲拳　　　　　　　Side fist thrust in a left bow stance

左弓步时，左膝垂直于脚背，右腿伸直，右脚全脚掌贴地，脚尖内扣；左拳收至腰间，右拳向前冲出，拳眼向上，臂与肩平，力达拳面；目视右拳。（图5-78）

要点：左脚开步时，身体重心先下沉，腰微右转，闭气蓄劲；侧冲拳时注重力起于根。

Keep the left knee perpendicular to the instep when forming the left bow stance. Keep the right leg straight, and the whole right foot on the ground, toes facing inward. Withdraw the left fist to the waist, and thrust the right fist forward, with the fist eye facing upward and arms at shoulder height. Convey the strength to the fist surface. Look at the right fist. (Fig. 5-78)

Key points: Lower the center of gravity before moving the left leg. Hold breadth and store up energy when turning the waist slightly to the right. Exert strength from the root when thrust fist from the side.

图 5-78　左弓步侧冲拳
Fig. 5-78 Side fist thrust in a left bow stance

2. 左弓步截桥　　　　　　　　Chop "bridge" in a left bow stance

左弓步时，左膝垂直于脚背，右腿伸直，右脚全脚掌贴地，脚尖内扣；左拳收至腰间，右臂微屈向前旋臂截桥，拳与肩同高，力达前臂端；目视右拳。（图5-79）

要点：上下肢动作完整一致，拧腰转胯迅速发力，力达前臂。

Keep the left knee perpendicular to the instep when forming the left bow stance. Keep the right leg straight, and the whole right foot on the ground, toes facing inward. Withdraw the left fist to the waist, bend the right arm slightly, and rotate it forward to chop the bridge, the fist at shoulder height, strength reaching to the end of the forearm. Look at the right fist. (Fig. 5-79)

Key points: Complete the upper and lower limbs movements in the same way and at the same time. Exert strength quickly when turning the waist and hips. Convey the strength to the forearm.

图 5-79　左弓步截桥
Fig. 5-79 Chop "bridge" in a left bow stance

3. 马步双切掌　　　　　　　　　　　Double-palm cutting in a horse stance

两腿半蹲成马步，上身直立，含胸拔背；两掌由左向前双切掌（右掌在上置于胸前、左掌在下置于腹前），两掌心向下，力达掌外沿；目视前方。（图5-80）

要点：发力于腰，两臂成圆，收腹、含胸。

Do a half squat with both legs and form a horse stance. Keep the upper body upright and back straight, and draw in chest. Both palms cut forward from the left side (the right palm placed on the top in front of the chest and the left one on the bottom in front of the abdomen), both palms facing downward. The strength reaches to the outer side of the palms. Look straight ahead. (Fig. 5-80)

Key points: Exert strength from the waist. Arms are formed as a round circle. Draw in belly and chest.

图 5-80　马步双切掌
Fig. 5-80 Double-palm cutting in a horse stance

4. 马步穿桥撑掌　　　　Cross "bridge" and hold up palm in a horse stance

左脚微后撤成高虚步，左掌经右臂下方向前画弧穿出，形成穿桥，右掌变拳收至右腰侧，拳心向上，目视左掌。两腿半蹲成马步，上身直立、含胸；左掌置于右胸前，掌心向外，右拳变掌斜向下方撑掌，掌心向下，力达掌根；目视右前方。（图5—81）

要点：穿桥要展腕、沉肘，右臂微用力回拉；马步撑掌要迅速拧腰转髋，同步完成。

Step back with the left foot slightly and form a high empty stance. The left palm crosses forward from under the right arm like drawing an arc, and then form a "bridge crossing". Change the right palm into a fist and draw it back to the right side of the waist, with the fist center facing upward. Look at the left palm. Do a half squat with both legs into a horse stance, with the upper body upright and the chest drew in. Place the left palm in front of the right side of the chest, the palm facing outward. Change the right fist into a palm, and then hold it up in an obliquely downward direction. Convey the strength to the palm root. Look at the right front side. (Fig. 5-81)

Key points: When crossing the bridge, extend wrists and lower elbows. Pull the right arm back with slight strength. When holding up palm in the horse stance, quickly twist the waist and turn hips at the same time.

图 5-81　马步穿桥撑掌
Fig. 5-81 Cross "bridge" and hold up palm in a horse stance

（二）指法 + 拳法 + 桥法 + 步法 + 步型
Techniques of Finger+Fist+Bridge+Step position+Step form

1. 马步双推指   Double-finger-pushing in a horse stance

两腿半蹲成马步，步型沉稳，圆裆敛臀；屈臂、合肘上挑至肩部，目视左侧；双指合肘收至腋下，掌心向前，目视右指；蓄劲向前推出，两臂刚劲有力，臂与肩平，力达指根，目视前方（图5-82）。下肢不动，上肢重复以上步骤，左、右手与之相反。

要点：马步沉稳，两臂刚劲有力，手法清晰。

Do a half squat with both legs and form a horse stance. Be steady with the stance, making the crotch round and holding back buttocks. Bend the arms, press the elbows inward and lift them up to the shoulders. Look at the left finger. Press elbows inward, put the two fingers down to the armpits, the palms facing forward. Look at the right finger. Store up energy and push them forward with strong and forceful arms at shoulder height. Convey the strength to the finger root. Look straight ahead (Fig. 5-82). Keep the lower limbs still, repeat the above steps for the upper limbs. The direction to look at the left or the right hand is opposite.

Key points: Keep the horse stance stable. Be strong and forceful with the arms. Make clear-cut movements of the hands.

图 5-82 马步双推指
Fig. 5-82 Double-finger-pushing in a horse stance

2. 右弓步架桥　　　　　　　　Build "bridge" in a right bow stance

右弓步时，右膝垂直于脚背，左腿伸直，左脚全脚掌贴地，脚尖内扣；两臂经胸前上架于头部斜上方，拳心向下，臂呈弧形，力达前臂；目视前方。（图5-83）

要点：半马步转弓步时，拧腰转胯迅速有力；架桥时，两臂内旋，力达前臂。

Keep the right knee perpendicular to the instep in the right bow stance. Keep the left leg straight, and the whole left foot on the ground, toes facing inward. Place both arms diagonally above the head through the chest, with the fist centers facing downward, and the arms in an arc shape. Convey the strength to the forearms, and look straight ahead. (Fig. 5-83)

Key points: When changing the half horse stance to the bow stance, twist the waist and turn the hips quickly and powerfully; when building the bridge, the arms are rotated inward, and the strength reaches the forearm.

图 5-83　右弓步架桥
Fig. 5-83　Build "bridge" in a right bow stance

3. 马步劈桥

Chop "bridge" in a horse stance

两腿半蹲成马步，圆裆敛臀，含胸拔背；右臂由上经体前内旋下劈，拳眼向上，置于身前，力达前臂，左拳变掌护于右臂内侧，掌心向右；目视右侧。（图5-84）

要点：步型的转换要迅速、稳健。劈桥时，以腰带臂，快速下劈。

Do a half squat with both legs and form a horse stance, making the crotch round, holding back buttocks, keeping the back straight, and drawing in chest. Chop the right arm down after it rotates in an upward-forward direction, and place it in front of the body, the fist eye facing upward. Convey the strength to the forearm. Place the left palm on the inner side of the right arm, with the palm facing to the right. Look at the right side. (Fig. 5-84)

Key points: Be fast and stable in changing step forms. Use the waist to drive arms when chopping the bridge. Chop down fast.

图 5-84　马步劈桥
Fig. 5-84　Chop "bridge" in a horse stance

（三）桥法＋腿法＋掌法＋步法＋步型
Techniques of Bridge+Leg+Palm+Step position+Step form

1. 劈桥左蹬脚　　　　　　　　　　Chop "bridge" and kick with left heel

侧身上步，两腿微屈，右脚外展；左臂由上向下外旋下劈，拳眼向上，置于体侧，力达前臂；右掌护于左臂内侧，掌心向左；目视左侧。右腿微屈支撑，左腿由屈到伸，向左侧蹬击，高与腰齐，力达脚跟，目视左侧。（图5-85）

要点：右脚上步劈桥时，左臂尽量外旋，屈肘下沉；蹬脚要由屈到伸，发力快脆。

Step up with the body side facing forward, bend the legs slightly, and turn the right foot out. Rotate the left arm outward in an top-down direction, and chop it down. Place the left arm on the body side with the fist eye facing upward, strength reaching the forearm. Place the right palm on the inner side of the left arm, the palm facing left. Look left. Bend the right leg slightly for support, extend the left leg from its bending position, and make a kicking strike to the left at the waist height. The strength reaches the heel. Look left. (Fig. 5-85)

Key points: When stepping forward with the right leg to chop the bridge, rotate the left arm outward as far as possible. Lower the elbow and bend it. Make a quick and clear-cut kicking strike when extending the leg from its bending position.

图 5-85　劈桥左蹬脚
Fig. 5-85 Chop "bridge" and kick with left heel

2. 右虚步分掌　　　　　Separate palms in a right empty stance

右虚步时，两腿接近半蹲，身体重心落于左腿，左脚全脚掌贴地，右脚屈膝前伸，脚尖点地；左拳变掌，两掌同时由外经面前交叉弧形分至左右两侧，掌与腹同高，掌心均向下，指尖向前，力达掌外沿；目视前方。（图5-86）

要点：虚步与分掌动作一致，分掌时力达掌根，收腹收胯。

In a right empty stance, the body position is close to a half squat. Put weight on the left leg, the whole left foot on the ground. Bend the right knee and move the right foot forward, tiptoes slightly touching the ground. Change the left fist into a palm, and then place palms on the left and right side respectively by forming a crossing arc in an outside-to-front direction. Hands are at belly height, palms facing down, and fingertips facing forward. The strength reaches to the outer side of the palms. Look straight ahead. (Fig. 5-86)

Key points: Form the empty stance and separate palms at the same time. The strength of separating palms reach the palm roots. Draw in belly and hips.

图 5-86　右虚步分掌
Fig. 5-86 Separate palms in a right empty stance

3. 马步撑掌   Hold up palm in a horse stance

两腿半蹲成马步，上身直立、含胸；左掌置于右胸前，掌心向外，右掌斜向下方撑掌，掌心向下，力达掌根；目视右前方。（图5-87）

要点：马步撑掌发力于腰。

Do a half squat with both legs and form a horse stance. Keep the upper body upright and draw in chest. Place the left palm in front of the right side of the chest, the palm facing outward. Hold up the right palm in an obliquely downward direction, the palm facing downward. Convey the strength to the palm root, and look ahead to the right side. (Fig. 5-87)

Key points: Exert strength from the waist when holding up palm in a horse stance.

图 5-87　马步撑掌
Fig. 5-87　Hold up palm in a horse stance

南拳段前八级   Nan Quan: Pre-Duan Level 8

（一）桥法＋拳法＋腿法＋步法＋掌法＋步型
Techniques of Bridge+Fist+Leg+Step position+Palm+Step form

1. 单蝶步劈桥   Chop "bridge" in a single fold stance

单蝶步时，左腿全蹲，右腿跪地，小腿及脚踝内侧贴地；右臂由上经体前外旋下劈，拳心向上，置于身前，力达前臂；左拳变掌护于右臂内侧，掌心向右；目视右侧。（图5-88）

要点：蝶步收胯下沉，劈桥时右臂尽量内旋，屈肘下沉。

In a single fold stance, do a full squat with the left leg, kneel on the ground with the right leg, and make the inner side of the calf and ankle touch the ground. Chop the right arm down after it rotates outward in an upward-forward direction, and place it in front of the body, the fist eye facing upward. Convey the strength to the forearm. Place the left palm on the inner side of the right arm, with the palm facing right. Look right. (Fig. 5-88)

Key points: Draw in and lower hips in the single fold stance. Make an internal rotation of the right arm as much as possible when chopping the bridge. Lower the elbow and bend it.

图 5-88　单蝶步劈桥
Fig. 5-88 Chop "bridge" in a single fold stance

2.马步双挂拳　　Two fists swing and strike from overhead in a horse stance

两腿半蹲成马步，上身直立，步型稳健；左掌变拳，两拳于头上交叉由内经面前向两侧弧形挂击，肘微屈，两拳心斜向上，力达拳背；目视右拳。（图5-89）

要点：挂拳时弧度可适当放大，但要注意手的位置，同时加强手、眼、步的配合。

Do a half squat with both legs and form a horse stance. Keep the upper body upright and the stance stable. Both fists cross over the head. Swing them down and make an arc-shape sweeping strike after the fists move from above the head through the front to sides. Bend the elbows slightly, both palms facing obliquely upward. Convey the strength the fist back. Look at the right fist. (Fig. 5-89)

Key points: When making a sweeping strike with the two separated fists, the arc can be appropriately big, but pay attention to the position of the hand forms, and at the same time strengthen the coordination of the hands, eyes and steps.

图 5-89　马步双挂拳
Fig. 5-89 Two fists swing and strike from overhead in a horse stance

3. 右蹬脚　　　　　　　　　　　　　　　　Kick with the right heel

左腿上步，两拳变掌同时由左经面前弧形收至右腰间成蝶掌，掌根相对（左上，右下）；右腿由屈到伸，立身拧腰向前蹬击，高与腰齐，力达脚跟；目视前方。（图5-90）

要点：蹬脚要由屈到伸，发力快脆，注意立身拧腰的动作要领。

Step forward with the left leg. Form a butterfly palm with both palms withdrawing to the waist in an arc shape from the left to the front, the palm roots facing each other (left upper side, right lower side). Extend the right leg from its bending position. Kick with heel at waist height while keeping the body upright and twisting the waist. Convey the strength to the heel. Look straight ahead. (Fig. 5-90)

Key points: Make a quick and clear-cut kicking when extending the leg from its bending position. Pay attention to the movement essentials of keeping the body upright and twisting the waist.

图 5-90　右蹬脚
Fig. 5-90 Kick with the right heel

4. 盖步   Gaibu (Forward-inserting step)

右腿落步，左脚经右脚向前上步，拧腰，脚尖外展，两腿屈膝交叉成盖步；同时腰微左转，两掌收于左侧成蝶掌，目视右侧。（图5-91）

要点：右腿落步与行走盖步时，注意结合身腰协调配合。

Step down with the right leg, and then the left foot steps forward through the right foot, twisting the waist and turning the toes out. Bend the knees and cross the legs to form a forward-inserting step; at the same time, turn the waist slightly to the left, withdrawing both palms on the left side to form a butterfly palm, and look right. (Fig. 5-91)

Key points: When stepping down with the right leg and stepping forward to form the forward-inserting step, pay attention to the coordination of the waist and body.

图 5-91　盖步
Fig. 5-91　Gaibu (Forward-inserting step)

5. 右骑龙步横切掌　　　　　Side palm cutting in a right dragon-riding stance

右脚上步，两腿屈膝成右骑龙步；同时腰微右转，两掌向前平推，左肘下沉，左掌心向上，右掌心向下，右臂呈弧形；目视前方。（图5-92）

要点：骑龙步步型须沉实稳重，推掌时借助左腿内旋和转腰的力量，发劲短促。

Step up forward with the right foot. Bend the knees to form a right dragon-riding stance while turning the waist slightly to the right, pushing palms forward, and lowering the left elbow, the left palm facing upward. Make the right palm face downward, and the right arm in an arc shape. Look straight ahead. (Fig. 5-92)

Key points: Be solid and stable when forming the dragon-riding stance. When pushing palms, use the strength of internal rotation of the left leg and waist turning to make a short burst of strength exertion.

图 5-92　右骑龙步横切掌
Fig. 5-92 Side palm cutting in a right dragon-riding stance

（二）指法 + 桥法 + 拳法 + 步法 + 格打 + 步型
Techniques of Finger+Bridge+Fist+Step position+ Grappling+Step form

1. 右弓步左右推指 　　　Left and right finger push in a right bow stance

身体右转90°，右腿接近半蹲成弓步，右膝垂直于脚背，左腿伸直，左脚全脚掌贴地，脚尖内扣。双单指置于躯干两侧，外旋臂向前水平屈伸，直臂置于体前；双单指水平回收至胸前，手心向下；双肘向下立圆置于腋下，双单指向左右两侧水平推出，两臂刚劲有力，力达掌根；目视左指。（图5-93）

要点：眼随手动，手法清晰，两臂刚劲有力。

Turn the body to the right at a 90-degree angle. Do a nearly half squat with the right leg to form a bow stance, the right knee perpendicular to the instep. Keep the left leg straight and the sole of the left foot on the ground, the toes facing inward. Place the two fingers on the sides of the torso, rotate and extend the external arm forward horizontally, and place the straight arm in front of the body. Withdraw the two fingers horizontally to the chest, with the palms facing down. Place the elbows under the armpits and form a vertical circle with them, pushing the two fingers to the left and right side horizontally, keeping the arms strong and powerful. Convey the strength to the palm roots, and look at the left finger. (Fig. 5-93)

Key points: Eyes follow the movement of hands. The hand techniques should be clear. Keep the arms strong and powerful.

图 5-93 右弓步左右推指
Fig. 5-93 Left and right finger push in a right bow stance

2. 右弓步圈桥沉桥　　Quanqiao (Move around the "bridge") and Chenqiao (Sink the "bridge") in a right bow stance

右腿接近半蹲成弓步，左右两臂伸直，以肘关节为轴，两前臂向后、上沿立圆圈绕，置于躯干左右两侧，目视左掌；沉桥时两臂由上向下屈肘下沉，力达前臂，目视左掌。（图5-94）

要点：左右圈桥时，分别按左手顺时针方向、右逆时针方向运行；沉桥时，以肘带腕，快速下沉，短促有力。

Form a bow stance by doing nearly a half squat with the right leg. Keep the left and right arm straight. Using the elbow joints as the axis, two forearms move around the vertical circle backwards and upward. Then place them on the sides of the torso. Look at the left palm. When sinking the bridge, bend elbows and sink them down from above. Convey the strength to the forearms. Look at the left palm. (Fig. 5-94)

Key points: When moving around the bridge with the two arms, the left hand moves clockwise, and the right one moves counterclockwise respectively. When sinking the bridge, use elbows to drive wrists. Make a quick, short and powerful sink.

图 5-94　右弓步圈桥沉桥
Fig. 5-94 Quanqiao (Move around the "bridge") and Chenqiao (Sink the "bridge") in a right bow stance

3. 挂盖拳   Guagaiquan (Fists swing overhead)

左脚向左前方上步，脚尖微扣，右腿伸直成左弓步；同时腰左转，双单指变拳，左拳随转体经上反臂挂至左后侧，臂伸直；右拳经上扣盖至体前，手臂自然下落，拳心向内；目视前方。（图5-95）

要点：挂盖时幅度宜大，以腰带臂，发力于腰。

Step up forward with the left foot to the left, toes slightly facing inward. Straighten the right leg and form a left bow stance. At the same time, change the two fingers to fists. The left fist follows the turning of the body and then hangs upside down on the left back side, the arm straight. Thump the right fist from the upper body to the front, the arm falling naturally and the fist center facing inward. Look straight ahead. (Fig. 5-95)

Key points: Use the waist to drive arms in guagaiquan with a large range of movements. Exert strength from the waist.

图 5-95　挂盖拳
Fig. 5-95 Guagaiquan (Fists swing overhead)

4. 退步格打   Step back to grapple

左、右脚依次向后退步成弓步，上身直立，含胸拔背；同时右、左臂由内向外依次挂挑格挡，拳心向里；随后右拳由腰间向前冲出，臂与肩平，力达拳面，左拳收至腰间，拳心向上；目视右拳。（图5-96）

要点：左脚退步时，应完成右、左拳的挂挑；右脚退步时与右冲拳一致，以加大右冲拳的力度。

Step back with left and right foot in turn and form a bow stance. Keep the upper body upright and back straight, and draw in chest. At the same time, lift the right and left arm in turn from inside out to grapple, the fist centers facing inwards. Then thrust the right fist straight forward, with the arm at shoulder height. Convey the strength to the fist surface. Withdraw the left fist to the waist, with the fist center facing upward. Look at the right fist. (Fig. 5-96)

Key points: Complete the lifting of the right and left fist before stepping back with the left foot. Step back with the right leg and thrust the right fist at the same time, so as to intensify the strength of thrusting the right fist.

图 5-96　退步格打
Fig. 5-96　Step back to grapple

5. 右弓步侧冲拳   Side fist thrust in a right bow stance

右脚向右侧移步，左脚随转胯蹬腿，成右弓步；同时身体右转，左拳向左侧冲出，拳眼向上，臂与肩平；右拳收至腰间，拳心向上；目视左拳。（图5-97）

要点：转右弓步时，注重腰髋部位的拧转与左蹬腿时的协调发力；侧冲拳与腰腿拧转发力同步完成。

Step to the right with the right foot, turn hips, and kick with the left heel to form a right bow stance. At the same time, turn the body to the right, and thrust the left fist forward from the left side, the fist eye facing upward, the arm at shoulder height. Withdraw the right fist to the waist, the fist center facing upward. Look at the left fist. (Fig. 5-97)

Key points: When forming the right bow stance, coordinate the strength exertion of turning the waist and hips and of kicking with the left heel. Complete the side fist thrust and strength exertion of turning the waist and leg at the same time.

图 5-97　右弓步侧冲拳
Fig. 5-97 Side fist thrust in a right bow stance

（三）指法＋步法＋掌法＋腿法＋步型
Techniques of Finger+Step position+Palm+Leg+Step form

1.右弓步单推指　　　　　　　　Single-finger-pushing in a right bow stance

身体右转90°，右腿接近半蹲成弓步，右膝垂直于脚背，左腿伸直，左脚全脚掌贴地，脚尖内扣。右拳收至腰间；左拳变单指向左侧推出，指尖向上，推指刚劲有力，臂与肩平，力达掌根；目视左手。（图5-98）

要点：转右弓步时，注重腰髋部位的拧转与左蹬腿时的协调发力；推指与腰腿拧转发力同步完成。

Turn the body to the right at a 90-degree angle. Do a nearly half squat with the leg to form a bow stance, the right knee perpendicular to the instep. Keep the left leg straight and the sole of the left foot on the ground, the toes facing inward. Withdraw the right fist to the waist, push the left single finger forward to the left, the fingertip facing upward. Push the finger forcefully, the arm at shoulder height. Convey the strength to the root of the palm, and look at the left hand. (Fig. 5-98)

Key points: When forming the right bow stance, coordinate the strength exertion of turning the waist and hips and of kicking with the left heel. Complete the finger pushing and strength exertion of turning the waist and leg at the same time.

图 5-98　右弓步单推指
Fig. 5-98 Single-finger-pushing in a right bow stance

2.左右麒麟步蝶掌　　　Butterfly palm with the left and right Qilin step

右麒麟步蝶掌：两脚依次向右、左斜横向交叉迈步，腿微屈，一脚脚尖外展，另一脚脚跟离地，重心下沉平稳。蝶掌掌根相对，置于躯干左右两侧，与步法同步运行（左脚在前，蝶掌置于左侧；右脚在前，蝶掌置于右侧）。弓步腿接近半蹲；两掌左上右下向前推出，两掌心向前，两掌根相距一定距离，力达掌根，目视两掌（图5-99）。左麒麟步蝶掌与右麒麟步蝶掌动作步骤相同，方向相反。

要点：左右上步为麒麟步，两腿交叉，弓步腿脚尖外展，另一脚跟离地，重心下沉平稳；两掌以肘关节为轴盘绕，幅度宜小，推掌时发力于腿。

For the butterfly palm with the right Qilin step: Make a obliquely horizontal cross step to the right, and to the left with the feet in turn. Bend the legs slightly, turning the toes of one foot out, and keeping the heel of another foot off the ground. Lower the center of gravity and make it stable, the palm roots facing each other and placed on the sides of the torso. Form the butterfly palm and the footwork at the same time (When the left foot is in the front, the butterfly palm is on the left side; when the right foot is in the front, the butterfly palm is on the right side). Do a near half squat when forming the bow stance. Push palms to a upper left and lower right side respectively, both palms facing forward. Keep a distance between the palms, and convey the strength to the palm roots. Look at the palms (Fig. 5-99). The butterfly palm with the left Qilin step is exactly the same with the butterfly palm with the right Qilin step, just in opposite direction.

Key points: The step-ups with the left and right leg are Qilin steps. Cross the legs, turn the toes of the bow-stance foot out, another heel off the ground. Be stable when lowering the center of gravity. Move the palms round by using the elbow joint as the axis with a small range of movements. Exert strength from legs when pushing palms.

图 5-99　左右麒麟步蝶掌
Fig. 5-99 Butterfly palm with the left and right Qilin step

3. 右蹬脚　　　　　　　　　　　　　　　　　Kick with the right heel

动作步骤和要点与段前八级第 1 个组合中的第 3 个动作一致。（图 5-100）

The movement steps and key points are the same as the third movement in the first combination of the Pre-duan Level 8. (Fig. 5-100)

图 5-100　右蹬脚
Fig. 5-100 Kick with the right heel

4. 马步撑掌   Hold up palm in a horse stance

动作步骤和要点与段前七级第 3 个组合中的第 3 个动作一致。（图 5-101）

The movement steps and key points are the same as the third movement in the third combination of the Pre-duan Level 7. (Fig. 5-101)

图 5-101　马步撑掌

Fig. 5-101　Hold up palm in a horse stance

南拳段前九级　　　　　Nan Quan: Pre-Duan Level 9

南拳段前九级
Nan Quan: Pre-
Duan Level 9

（一）拳法＋步法＋手法＋掌法＋腿法＋虎爪＋步型
Techniques of Fitst+Step position+Hand+Palm+Leg+
Tiger claw+Step form

1.右弓步架打　　　　Strike out one fist with the other upheld in a right bow stance

右脚向右前方上步成弓步，右腿接近半蹲，右膝垂直于脚背，左腿伸直，左脚全脚掌贴地，脚尖内扣；同时右拳上架于头前上方，左拳向右前方立冲拳，拳眼向上；目视左拳。（图5-102）

要点：左脚后蹬成弓步时与架冲拳要同步到位，步型要稳，架打时左腿要撑紧。

Step forward to the right with the right foot and form a bow stance, with the right leg into a near half squat. Keep the right knee perpendicular to the instep. Keep the left leg straight, and the sole of the left foot on the ground, the toes facing inward. At the same time, place the right fist above the head, and strike out the left fist on its standing position straight forward, with the fist eye facing upward. Look at the left fist. (Fig. 5-102)

Key points: When the left foot is stepped back into a bow stance, it should be synchronized with the upholding and striking of the fists. Keep the stance stable. The left leg should be tightened when striking.

图 5-102　右弓步架打
Fig. 5-102　Strike out one fist with the other upheld in a right bow stance

2.左右弓步抛拳　　　　　　　　Throw fist in a left and right bow stance

左弓步抛拳：左腿接近半蹲成左弓步，左膝垂直于脚背，右腿伸直，右脚全脚掌贴地，脚尖内扣。左臂经下摆至后方成平拳，拳心向下；右直臂由右经下、左方位，向正前方弧形抛起，力达前臂端，拳心向后，目视右前方。右弓步抛拳与左弓步抛拳动作步骤相同，方向相反。（图5-103）

要点：左、右脚斜向横线上步，臂的抡摆幅度宜大，以腰带臂，前踩与后蹬对称用力。

Throw fist in a left bow stance: Do a near half squat with the left leg and form a left bow stance. Keep the left knee perpendicular to the instep, the right leg straight, and the sole of the right leg on the ground, the toes facing inward. Swing the left arm from the bottom and raise it to the back side to form a flat fist, with the fist center facing down. Throw the right arm straight ahead after it passes in an arc shape in a right-down-left direction. Convey the strength to the end of the forearm, the fist eye facing backward. Look ahead to the right. The fist throw in a right bow stance is exactly the same with the fist throw in a left bow stance, just in opposite direction. (Fig. 5-103)

Key points: Step forward with the left or right foot to the left or right side in a straight line. Swing the arm with a large range of movements, using the waist to drive the arm. Exert symmetrical strength on stepping forward and kicking backward with heel.

图 5-103　左右弓步抛拳
Fig. 5-103 Throw fist in a left and right bow stance

3. 右左虚步鹤嘴手　　Crane's beak (Form a crane beak by using the hand) in a right and left empty stance

右虚步鹤嘴手：右虚步接近半蹲，身体重心落于左腿，全脚掌贴地，右腿屈膝前伸，脚尖点地。右拳变掌以腕为轴沿逆时针方向绕一圈后变鹤嘴手，指尖向外，置于耳侧，上臂与前臂夹紧；左拳变鹤嘴手向右前方啄击，臂微屈，指尖向右前方，力达指尖，目视左手。左虚步鹤嘴手与右虚步鹤嘴手动作步骤相同，方向相反。（图5-104）

要点：鹤嘴手啄击时手行弧线，幅度宜小，以腰带臂左右转动，指尖斜向外，意指啄击太阳穴。

Crane's peak in a right empty stance: Do a near half squat when forming the right empty stance. Put the body weight on the left leg, with the whole sole on the ground. Bend the right knee and extend it forward, tiptoes slightly touching the ground.Change the right fist into a palm and move it around the wrist in a counterclockwise direction and then turn it into a crane's peak, fingers pointing outside and placed beside the ear, and the upper arm and forearm clamped. The left crane's peak pecks forward to the right. Bend the arm slightly, fingers facing forward to the right, and strength reaching to the fingertips. Look at the left hand. The crane's peak in the left empty stance is exactly the same with the crane's peak in the right empty stance, just in opposite direction. (Fig. 5-104)

Key points: When the crane's peak is pecking, the hand moves in an arc with a small range of movements. Use the waist to drive the arm to turn left or right. Fingers face obliquely outward, meaning pecking at the temple.

图 5-104　右左虚步鹤嘴手
Fig. 5-104 Crane's beak (Form a crane beak by using the hand) in a right and left empty stance

4. 分掌弹踢　　　　　　　　　Separate palms and do a hook kick

两掌同时由上经身前交叉弧形分至左右两侧，手与腹同高，掌心均向下，指尖向前，力达掌外沿；弹腿由屈到伸，脚尖绷直，向前快速有力踢弹，力达脚尖；目视前方。（图5-105）

要点：分掌与弹踢动作一致，发力快脆，收腹收胯。

The two palms from a crossing arc when they pass in an up-front direction, and then are separated simultaneously on the left and right side respectively, hands at belly height, the palms facing down, the fingertips facing forward, and the strength reaching the outer edge of the palms. When doing a hook kick, extend the leg from its bending position, stretch the foot, and kick forward quickly and powerfully, the strength reaching to the tiptoes. Look straight ahead. (Fig. 5-105)

Key points: Separate palms and do a hook kick at the same time. Exert strength in a fast and smooth way. Draw in belly and hips.

5. 马步撑掌　　　　　　　　　Hold up palm in a horse stance

动作步骤和要点与段前七级第 3 个组合中的第 3 个动作一致。（图5-106）

The movement steps and key points are the same as the third movement in the third combination of the Pre-duan Level 7. (Fig. 5-106)

图 5-105　分掌弹踢　　　　　　　　图 5-106　马步撑掌
Fig. 5-105　Separate palms and do a hook kick　　Fig. 5-106　Hold up palm in a horse stance

6. 跪步双虎爪　　　　　　Double tiger claw in a kneeling stance

两脚同时起跳，右、左脚依次落地（右脚在后、左脚在前）；两掌变双虎爪由左至右立圆收于腰两侧；跪步时左腿屈膝下蹲，右腿屈膝下跪，膝关节悬空，脚跟离地，臀部贴坐小腿上；双虎爪向左前方平推，臂与肩平；目视前方。（图5-107）

要点：几个分解动作要连贯；左脚适当向前跨步，右脚跟进；跪步时含胸拔背，两臂用力，力达爪指。

Take off with both feet at the same time, and land on the right and left foot in turn (right foot behind, left foot in front). Withdraw both tiger claws from left to right, moving in a vertical circle, and place them on both sides of the waist. When form a kneeling stance, bend the left leg and squat down, and bend the right leg and kneel down. Keep knee joints in the air, heels off the ground, and buttocks on the calf. Push both claws forward to the left, arms at shoulder height. Look straight ahead. (Fig. 5-107)

Key points: The movement segments should be completed coherently. Step forward moderately with the left foot, and the right foot follows up. In the kneeling stance, keep the upper body upright and back straight, and draw in chest. Exert strength with both arms, and convey strength to the fingers of the claws.

图 5-107　跪步双虎爪
Fig. 5-107 Double tiger claw in a kneeling stance

（二）腿法＋拳法＋指法＋步法＋掌法＋格打＋桥法＋步型
Techniques of Leg+Fist+Finger+Step position+Palm+Grappling+
Bridge+Step form

1. 左蹬腿右冲拳　　　　　　　　Kick with the left heel and thrust right fist

右脚上步，左腿由屈到伸向前蹬出，与腰同高；同时左拳变掌附在右胸前，右拳向前冲立拳，拳眼向上；目视前方。（图5-108）

要点：蹬腿与冲拳动作要同步到位，蹬腿时力达脚跟，冲拳时力达拳面。

Step forward with the right foot, and kick with the left heel at waist height after extending the left leg from its bending position; at the same time, change the left fist into a palm and attach it to the right side of the chest. Thrust the right fist forward on its standing position, with the fist eye facing upward. Look straight ahead. (Fig. 5-108)

Key points: When kicking with heel, it should be synchronized with fist thrusting. The strength reaches the heel when kicking, and the fist surface when thrusting.

图 5-108　左蹬腿右冲拳
Fig. 5-108 Kick with the left heel and thrust right fist

2.跪步盖拳　　　　　　　　　Gaiquan (Thrust down fist) in a kneeling stance

跪步时，左腿屈膝下蹲，右腿屈膝下跪，膝关节悬空，脚跟离地，臀部贴坐小腿上；右臂由后经上、前立圆直臂下盖至裆下，力达拳锋，左掌护于右胸前，掌心向外；目视右拳。（图5-109）

要点：动作连贯，盖拳抡臂动作弧度宜大，跪步时右腿微外展，含胸拔背。

When form a kneeling stance, bend the left leg and squat down, and bend the right leg and kneel down. Keep knee joints in the air, heels off the ground, and buttocks on the calf. Move the right arm and from a vertical circle in a back-up-front direction, extend the arm, and thrust down the right fist to the crotch. Exert strength to the fist peak. Place the left palm on the right side of the chest, with the palm facing outward. Look at the right fist. (Fig. 5-109)

Key points: Complete the movements smoothly. Swing the arm and thrust down the fist with a large range of movements. Turn the right leg slightly outward in the kneeling stance. Keep the upper body upright and back straight.

图 5-109　跪步盖拳
Fig. 5-109 Gaiquan (Thrust down fist) in a kneeling stance

3. 骑龙步单推指　　　　Single-finger-pushing in a dragon-riding stance

骑龙步时，右腿接近半蹲，全脚掌贴地，左腿下跪，小腿呈水平位，脚跟提起，膝关节悬空；右拳收至腰间，左掌变单指向左侧推出，指尖向上，推指刚劲有力，臂与肩平，力达掌根；目视左手。（图5-110）

要点：马步转骑龙步时，注重腰髋部位的拧转发力；推指应与拧腰转胯同步完成。

When forming the dragon-riding stance, do a near half squat with the right leg, the whole right foot on the ground. Kneel down with the left leg. Keep the calf horizontal, lift the left heel, and keep the knee joint in the air. Withdraw the right fist to the waist, pushing the left single finger to the left side, the fingertip facing upward. Make a strong and powerful push of the finger, the arm at shoulder height and the strength reaching the palm root. Look at the left hand. (Fig. 5-110)

Key points: When changing from the horse stance to the dragon-riding stance, pay attention to the twisting strength exertion of the waist and hips. Push the finger and twist the waist and hips at the same time.

图 5-110　骑龙步单推指
Fig. 5-110 Single-finger-pushing in a dragon-riding stance

4. 右麒麟步蝶掌　　　　　　　　Butterfly palm with the right Qilin step

动作步骤和要点与段前八级第3个组合中第2个动作一致。（图 5-111）

The movement steps and key points are the same as the second movement in the third combination of the Pre-duan Level 8. (Fig. 5-111)

图 5-111　右麒麟步蝶掌
Fig. 5-111 Butterfly palm with the right Qilin step

5. 退步格打　　　　　　　　　　　　Step back to grapple

动作步骤和要点与段前八级第 2 个组合中的第 4 个动作一致。（图 5-112）

The movement steps and key points are the same as the fourth movement in the second combination of the Pre-duan Level 8. (Fig. 5-112)

图 5-112　退步格打
Fig. 5-112 Step back to grapple

6.弓步滚桥   Gunqiao（"Bridge" rolling）in a bow stance

右腿向右侧迈出成弓步，身体右转90°；同时左前臂由内向外旋转滚出，沉肩坠肘，力达前臂外侧，右臂屈肘水平收至右胸前；目视左侧。（图5-113）

要点：练习滚桥时，技法要清晰，力达前臂外侧；转右弓步时，注重腰髋部位的拧转与左蹬腿时的协调发力；滚桥与右弓步转腰发力须同步完成。

Step aside with the right foot into a bow stance. Turn the body to the right at a 90-degree angle. At the same time, the left forearm rolls forward from the inside out. Lower the shoulders and elbows. Convey the strength to the outside of the forearm. Bend the right arm, and draw it back horizontally to the front of the chest. Look left. (Fig. 5-113)

Key points: When practicing bridge rolling, make clear of the movements. The strength should reach the outside of the forearm. When forming the right bow stance, coordinate the strength exertion of turning the waist and hips and of kicking with the left heel. Complete the bridge rolling and strength exertion of turning the waist and leg in the right bow stance at the same time.

图 5-113 弓步滚桥
Fig. 5-113 Gunqiao ("Bridge" rolling) in a bow stance

（三）虎爪 + 手法 + 独立步 + 指法 + 腿法 + 桥法 + 步型

Techniques of Tiger claw+Hand+Standing on a singer foot+
Finger+Leg+Bridge+Step form

1.跪步双虎爪   Double tiger claw in a kneeling stance

动作步骤和要点与段前九级第 1 个组合中的第 6 个动作一致。（图 5-114）

The movement steps and key points are the same as the sixth movement in the first combination of the Pre-duan Level 9. (Fig. 5-114)

图 5-114　跪步双虎爪
Fig. 5-114　Double tiger claw in a kneeling stance

2. 右左虚步鹤嘴手   Crane's beak in a right and left empty stance

动作要求和要点与段前九级第 1 个组合中的第 3 个动作一致。（图 5-115）

The movement steps and key points are the same as the third movement in the first combination of the Pre-duan Level 9. (Fig. 5-115)

图 5-115 右左虚步鹤嘴手
Fig. 5-115 Crane's beak in a right and left empty stance

3. 独立步推指   Push finger on a single foot

右腿支撑，左腿屈腿提膝，脚尖绷直内扣；右鹤嘴手变拳抱于腰间，左鹤嘴手变单指向左腿内侧斜下方推出，指尖向上，掌心斜向下，力达掌根；目视左指。（图5-116）

要点：屈腿、推指与目视方向要一致。

Use the right leg for support. Bend the left leg, raise the knee, and stretch the foot, toes facing inward. Change the right Crane's peak into a fist and place it on the waist. Change the left Crane's peak into a single-finger position, and push the finger out obliquely below the inner side of the left leg, the index finger up, the palm facing obliquely down, and the strength reaching the palm root. Look at the left finger. (Fig. 5-116)

Key points: Bend the leg, push the finger and look in the same direction.

图 5-116　独立步推指
Fig. 5-116 Push finger on a single foot

4.分掌弹踢　　　　　　　　　　　　Separate palms and do a hook kick

动作步骤和要点与段前九级第 1 个组合中的第 4 个动作一致。（图 5-117）

The movement steps and key points are the same as the fourth movement in the first combination of the Pre-duan Level 9. (Fig. 5-117)

图 5-117　分掌弹踢
Fig. 5-117 Separate palms and do a hook kick

5. 右弓步架桥   Build "bridge" in a right bow stance

动作步骤和要点与段前七级第 2 个组合中的第 2 个动作一致。（图 5–118）

The movement steps and key points are the same as the second movement in the second combination of the Pre-duan Level 7. (Fig. 5-118)

图 5–118 右弓步架桥
Fig. 5-118 Build "bridge" in a right bow stance

6. 马步劈桥   Chop "bridge" in a horse stance

动作步骤和要点与段前七级第 2 个组合中的第 3 个动作一致。（图 5–119）

The movement steps and key points are the same as the third movement in the second combination of the Pre-duan Level 7. (Fig. 5-119)

图 5–119 马步劈桥
Fig. 5-119 Chop "bridge" in a horse stance

南拳段位考评技术内容

Duanwei Grading System
for Nan Quan

一段南拳 Nan Quan: Grade 1

一段南拳
Nan Quan:
Grade 1

动作名称

预备势

第一段

1. 虚步冲拳推掌
2. 虚步抱拳
3. 左弓步侧冲拳
4. 马步连环掌
5. 马步双推指
6. 右弓步蝶掌
7. 左弓步冲拳

第二段

8. 马步冲拳
9. 回身半马步截桥
10. 右弓步冲拳
11. 左虚步穿桥
12. 马步冲拳
13. 转身马步劈拳
14. 回身弓步双推掌
15. 虚步冲拳推掌
16. 虚步抱拳

收势

Names of the Movements

Preparatory posture

Section 1

1. Thrust fist and push palm in an empty stance
2. Hold fist and palm together in an empty stance
3. Side fist thrust in a left bow stance
4. Lianhuanzhang (Linked palm) in a horse stance
5. Double-finger-pushing in a horse stance
6. Butterfly palm in a right bow stance
7. Thrust fist in a left bow stance

Section 2

8. Thrust fist in a horse stance
9. Jieqiao (Cut "bridge") with the body turning around in a half horse stance
10. Thrust fist in a right bow stance
11. Cross "bridge" in a left empty stance
12. Thrust fist in a horse stance
13. Straight-arm chop with the body turning in a horse stance
14. Push palms with the body turning around in a bow stance
15. Thrust fist and push palm in an empty stance
16. Hold fist and palm together in an empty stance

Closing posture

预备势 Preparatory posture

（1）两脚并步，直腿站立；直臂，两掌贴靠于两腿外侧；目视前方。［图6-1（1）］

（2）两腿不动，两掌握拳提抱于腰间，拳心向上；目视前方。［图6-1（2）］

要点：挺膝，夹腿，收腹，敛臀，立腰，提神降气。

(1) Stand with both feet together with straight legs. Place both palms against the outside of the two legs, arms straight. Look straight ahead. [Fig. 6-1(1)]

(2) Keep the legs still. Change palms into fists and withdraw them to the waist, the fist centers facing upward. Look straight ahead. [Fig. 6-1(2)]

Key points: Straighten knees. Squeeze legs togeher. Draw in belly, hold back battocks and keep the waist straight up. Keep spirits up and lower the qi.

图 6-1　预备势（1）　　　　图 6-1　预备势（2）
Fig. 6-1 Preparatory posture (1)　　Fig. 6-1 Preparatory posture (2)

第一段　Section 1

1. 虚步冲拳推掌　　　　　Thrust fist and push palm in an empty stance

（1）右脚向右前上步，脚尖外展，膝微屈；同时腰微右转，右拳提至右胸前，拳心向下；左拳变掌弧形向上摆至右胸前，掌指向上，掌心与右拳面相对；目视右拳。［图6-2（1）］

（2）左脚向前上半步，脚尖点地成左虚步；同时腰微左转，右拳向前冲拳、左掌向前推掌，两臂伸直与肩同高、同宽，左掌心与右拳面均向前；目视前方。［图6-2（2）］

要点：右脚与左脚上步时重心下沉，虚实分明，冲拳、推掌发力于腰，眼随手动。

(1) Step forward to the right with the right foot, toes turning out and the knee slightly bent. At the same time, turn the waist slightly right, and lift the right fist to the right side of the chest, the fist center facing downward. Swing the left palm in an arc shape to the right side of the chest, the palm fingers facing upward, and the palm center facing the right fist surface. Look at the right fist. [Fig. 6-2(1)]

(2) Make a half step forward with the left foot. The tiptoes slightly touch the ground and form a left empty stance. At the same time, turn the waist slightly to the left, thrust the right fist and push the left palm forward. Straighten both arms at shoulder height and shoulder-width apart. Both the left palm center and the right fist surface face forward. Look straight ahead. [Fig. 6-2(2)]

Key points: When stepping with the right and left foot, lower the center of gravity. Differentiate between "Xu" and "Shi" (Make clear of empty and solid movements). Exert strength when thrusting the fist and pushing the palm. Eyes follow the movement of hands.

图 6-2　虚步冲拳推掌（1）
Fig. 6-2 Thrust fist and push palm in an empty stance (1)

图 6-2　虚步冲拳推掌（2）
Fig. 6-2 Thrust fist and push palm in an empty stance (2)

2. 虚步抱拳　　　　　　　Hold fist and palm together in an empty stance

（1）步不动；左掌变拳，两拳随屈肘拉至右侧胸前，拳面相对；同时腰微右转；目视两拳。［图6-3（1）］

（2）步仍不动，腰微左转；两臂外提，两拳经上向前反臂挂收于腰间，拳心向上；目视前方。［图6-3（2）］

要点：虚步稳固，以腰带臂。

(1) Keep the stance. Change the left palm into a fist. Bend elbows, and then pull both fists to the right side of the chest, the fist surfaces facing each other. At the same time, turn the waist slightly to the right. Look at both fists. [Fig. 6-3(1)]

(2) Still keep the stance. Turn the waist slightly to left. Lift both arms ourward, and then hang both fists upside down on the waist after moving them in an up-front direction, the palm centers facing upward. Look straight ahead. [Fig. 6-3(2)]

Key points: Keep the empty stance stable. Use the waist to drive arms.

图 6-3　虚步抱拳（1）
Fig. 6-3 Hold fist and palm
together in an empty stance (1)

图 6-3　虚步抱拳（2）
Fig. 6-3 Hold fist and palm
together in an empty stance (2)

3. 左弓步侧冲拳 　　　　　　　Side fist thrust in a left bow stance

（1）左脚向左侧开步，两腿屈膝半蹲成半马步；同时腰微右转，左拳变掌由左侧经面前盖至右胸前，掌心向右；目视左掌。［图6-4（1）］

(1) Step to the left with the left foot. Bend the knees and do a half squat to form a half horse stance. At the same time, turn the waist slightly to the right. Chang the left fist into a palm, and thrust it from the left side through the front to the right side of the chest, the palm facing right. Look at the left palm. [Fig. 6-4(1)]

图 6-4　左弓步侧冲拳（1）
Fig. 6-4 Side fist thrust in a left bow stance (1)

（2）右脚蹬地，右腿内转挺膝伸直成左弓步；同时，腰微左转，右拳向右侧冲出，拳眼向上，臂与肩平；左掌变拳收至腰间，拳心向上；目视右拳，同时发声"嗨"。［图6-4（2）］

要点：半马步盖掌为蓄劲，腰微右转，重心略偏于右腿；弓步冲拳时注重蹬脚、扣膝、合胯、转腰，爆发性用劲。

(2) Form a left bow stance after pushing the right foot against the ground and turning the right leg inward before straightening the knee. At the same time, turn the waist slightly to the left, and thrust the right fist to the right, the fist eye facing upward and the arm at shoulder height. Change the left palm into a fist and withdraw it to the waist, the palm center facing upward. Look at the right fist, and make an utterance of "hi" at the same time. [Fig. 6-4(2)]

Key points: Store up energy when thrusting the palm down in a half horse stance. Turn the waist slightly to the right, and put a little more weight on the right leg. When thrusting fist in the horse stance, kick with heel, twist the knees, turn the waist and hips to exert explosive strength.

图 6-4　左弓步侧冲拳（2）
Fig. 6-4 Side fist thrust in a left bow stance (2)

4. 马步连环掌　　　　　　Lianhuanzhang (Linked palm) in a horse stance

（1）右脚向左踏一小步，两腿屈膝成马步；同时腰微左转，两拳变掌，右掌收至左腰侧，置于左掌之上，两掌心均向上；目视右掌。［图6-5（1）］

（2）马步不动；两掌以小指侧为力点同时向前击出，右掌与胸同高，左掌与腹同高，两掌心均向下，两臂微屈；目视右掌。［图6-5（2）］

要点：马步沉稳，发力于腰。

(1) Take a small step to the left with the right foot, and then bend both knees to form a horse stance. At the same time, turn the waist slightly to the left. Change both fists into palms, draw the right palm back to the left side of the waist, and place it on the left palm, both palms facing upward. Look at the right palm. [Fig. 6-5(1)]

(2) Stay in a horse stance. Use the sides of both little fingers as the point of exerting strength and push them forward at the same time. The right palm is at chest height, the left one at belly height, both palms facing downward, and both arms slightly bend. Look at the right palm. [Fig. 6-5(2)]

Key points: Keep the horse stance stable. Exert strength from the waist.

图 6-5　马步连环掌（1）
Fig. 6-5 Lianhuanzhang (Linked palm) in a horse stance (1)

图 6-5　马步连环掌（2）
Fig. 6-5 Lianhuanzhang (Linked palm) in a horse stance (2)

5. 马步双推指　　　　　Double-finger-pushing in a horse stance

（1）马步不动；左掌由下经右臂内侧弧形挑至左肩前，掌指向上，肘下沉；目视左掌。［图6-6（1）］

(1) Stay in a horse stance. Lift the left palm from the bottom through the inner side of the right arm to the front of the left shoulder, the palm fingers facing upward. Lower the elbow. Look at the left palm. [Fig. 6-6(1)]

图 6-6　马步双推指（1）
Fig. 6-6 Double-finger-pushing in a horse stance (1)

（2）右掌经外向下沿左臂内侧弧形挑至右肩前，掌指向上，肘下沉；两臂与肩同高、同宽；目视前方。［图6-6（2）］

(2) Lift the right palm from the outside to the inside of the left arm in an arc to the front of the right shoulder, the palm fingers facing upward. Lower the elbow. Keep arms at shoulder height, shoulder-width apart. Look straight ahead. [Fig. 6-6(2)]

图 6-6　马步双推指（2）
Fig. 6-6 Double-finger-pushing in a horse stance (2)

（3）马步保持不动；两掌变单指手，翘指坐腕，手心向前；目视前方。[图6-6（3）]

(3) Still keep the stance. Change both palms into the single-finger position, lowering the wrists and keeping the two fingers upright. Both palms face forward. Look straight ahead. [Fig. 6-6(3)]

图 6-6　马步双推指（3）
Fig. 6-6 Double-finger-pushing in a horse stance(3)

（4）两臂屈肘，两指挑至两肩上，两手心斜向上，两肘正对前方；目视右肘。[图6-6（4）]

(4) Bend the elbows. Lift the two fingers to the shoulders, both palms facing obliquely upward. Both elbows face forward. Look at the right elbow. [Fig. 6-6(4)]

图 6-6　马步双推指（4）
Fig. 6-6 Double-finger-pushing in a horse stance(4)

（5）两肘下沉，两指收至腰侧，手心斜向前下方；目视左指。［图 6-6（5）］

(5) Lower the elbows, and draw the two fingers back to the waist, with both palms facing obliquely downward. Look at the left finger. [Fig. 6-6(5)]

图 6-6　马步双推指（5）
Fig. 6-6 Double-finger-pushing in a horse stance(5)

（6）马步仍不动；两指用劲慢慢向前推出，臂与肩平，沉肘、坐腕、翘指；目视前方。［图6-6（6）］

(6) Still stay in the horse stance. Exert strength with the two fingers and push them forward slowly. The arms are at shoulder height. Lower the wrists and keep the two fingers upright. Look straight ahead. [Fig. 6-6(6)]

图 6-6　马步双推指（6）
Fig. 6-6 Double-finger-pushing in a horse stance(6)

要点：马步沉稳，两臂刚劲有力，手法清晰。

Key points: Keep the horse stance stable. Be strong and forceful with the arms. Make clear-cut movements of the hands.

6. 右弓步蝶掌   Butterfly palm in a right bow stance

（1）右脚向前上步，两腿屈膝半蹲，重心偏于左腿成半马步；同时腰微左转，两指手变掌随屈肘收于左腰侧，右掌在上，掌心向左；左掌在下，掌心向前，两掌成左侧蝶掌；目视左前方。［图6-7（1）］

(1) Step forward with the right foot. Bend the knees and do a half squat. Put a little more weight on the left leg and then form a half horse stance. At the same time, turn the waist slightly to the left, change back to palms from the two-single-finger position, and withdraw them to the left side of the waist, with the right palm on the top and facing left. Placed on the bottom, the left palm faces forward to form a left-sided butterfly palm. Look forward to the left. [Fig. 6-7(1)]

图 6-7 　右弓步蝶掌（1）
Fig. 6-7　Butterfly palm in a right bow stance (1)

（2）左脚蹬地，左腿内转挺膝成右弓步；同时腰微右转，两掌向前推出，右掌在上，掌指向上，左掌在下，掌指向下，两掌相距20～30厘米；目视前方。［图6-7（2）］

(2) Push the left foot against the ground. Turn the left leg inward and straighten the knee into a right bow stance. At the same time, turn the waist slightly to the right, and push both palms forward, with the right palm on the top and fingers facing upward. The left palm is on the bottom, fingers facing downward. Keep the distance between the two palms 20-30 cm. Look straight ahead. [Fig. 6-7(2)]

图 6-7　右弓步蝶掌（2）
Fig. 6-7 Butterfly palm in a right bow stance (2)

要点：右脚上步沉稳，蝶掌时力发于根。

Key points: Make a steady step-up with the right foot. Exert strength from the root when forming the butterfly palm.

7. 左弓步冲拳　　　　　　　　　　　Thrust fist in a left bow stance

（1）左脚向前上步，两腿屈膝半蹲，重心偏于右腿成半马步；同时腰微右转，右掌变拳收于腰间，拳心向上；左掌略经外弧形扣握于左侧，变拳心向下，拳眼斜向内；目视左拳。［图6-8（1）］

(1) Step forward with the left foot. Bend the knees and do a half squat. Put a little more weight on the right leg and then form a half horse stance. At the same time, turn the waist slightly to the right. Change the right palm into a fist and withdraw it to the waist, with the fist center facing upward. Move the left palm in an arc to the left and change it into a fist, with the fist center facing downward, and the fist eye facing obliquely inward. Look at the left fist. [Fig. 6-8(1)]

图 6-8　左弓步冲拳（1）
Fig. 6-8 Thrust fist in a left bow stance (1)

（2）右脚蹬地，右腿内转挺膝伸直成左弓步；同时腰微左转，右拳直线向前冲出，臂与肩平，拳心向下；左拳收抱于腰间，拳心向上；目视前方。［图6-8（2）］

(2) Form a left bow stance after pushing the right foot against the ground, and turning the right leg inward before straightening the knee. At the same time, turn the waist slightly to the left, and thrust the right fist straight ahead, the arm at shoulder height, and the fist center facing downward. Withdraw the left fist to the waist, with the fist center facing upward. Look straight ahead. [Fig. 6-8(2)]

图 6-8　左弓步冲拳（2）
Fig. 6-8 Thrust fist in a left bow stance (2)

要点：左脚上步沉稳，半马步时转腰、闭气蓄劲，冲拳时力起于根（右脚），爆发性用劲。

Key points: Make a steady step-up with the left foot. Turn the waist, hold breadth, and store up energy when forming the half horse stance. Exert explosive strength from the root (the right foot) when thrusting fist.

第二段　Section 2

8. 马步冲拳　　　　　　　　　　　　　　Thrust fist in a horse stance

右脚微外转，右腿屈膝成马步；同时腰微右转，左拳从腰间随转体向左侧冲出，拳眼向上，臂与肩平；右拳收抱于腰间，拳心向上；目视左拳。（图6-9）

要点：转腰、冲拳与收拳要一致，力发于腰。

Turn the right foot slightly out, bend the right knee and form a horse stance. At the same time, turn the waist slightly to the right, and thrust the left fist out to the left from the waist with the turning of the body, the fist eye facing upward and the arms at shoulder height. Withdraw the right fist to the waist, the fist center facing upward. Look at the left fist. (Fig. 6-9)

Key points: Turn the waist, thrust the left fist and withdraw the right fist at the same time. Exert strength from the waist.

图 6-9　马步冲拳
Fig. 6-9 Thrust fist in a horse stance

9. 回身半马步截桥

Jieqiao (Cut "bridge") with the body turning around in a half horse stance

右脚向右后移动半步，两腿屈膝半蹲，重心偏于左腿，成半马步；同时腰向右转约 45°，右拳从腰间随屈臂提起，经胸前向右侧截劈，拳心向下，力达前臂尺骨侧（小指一侧）；左拳收抱于腰间，拳心向上；目视右拳。（图6-10）

要点：移步与转体、截桥一致，右臂的运行幅度宜小。

Make a half-step backward with the right foot. Bend the knees and do a half squat. Put a little more waist on the left leg and then form a half horse stance. At the same time, turn the weight slightly to the right at a 45-degree angle. Lift the right fist from the waist with the bending of the arm and cut it to the right side through the front of the chest, the fist center facing down. Convey the strength to the ulnar side of forearm (the side of the little finger). Draw back the left fist to the waist, the fist center facing upward. Look at the right fist. (Fig. 6-10)

Key points: Move the foot, turn the body and cut the bridge at the same time. Move the right arm with a small range of movements.

图 6-10　回身半马步截桥
Fig. 6-10 Jieqiao (Cut "bridge") with the body turning around in a half horse stance

10. 右弓步冲拳　　　　　　　　　Thrust fist in a right bow stance

左脚蹬地，左腿内转挺膝伸直成右弓步；同时左拳从腰间直线向前冲拳，拳心向下，臂与肩平；右拳收抱于腰间，拳心向上；目视左拳。（图6-11）

要点：注重左腿的蹬转，力发于根，爆发性用劲。

Push the left foot against the ground, turn the left leg inward and straighten the knee to form a right bow stance. At the same time, thrust the left fist straight ahead from the waist, with the fist center facing down and the arm at shoulder height. Withdraw the right fist to the waist, with the fist center facing upward. Look at the left fist. (Fig. 6-11)

Key points: Pay attention to the pushing and turning of the left leg. Exert explosive strength from the root.

图 6-11　右弓步冲拳
Fig. 6-11 Thrust fist in a right bow stance

11. 左虚步穿桥   Cross "bridge" in a left empty stance

左脚向前上步，脚尖贴地成左虚步；同时右拳变掌沿左臂下向前穿出，掌心由向下变斜向前，掌指向前，右肘微屈下沉；左拳收抱于腰间，拳心向上；目视右掌。（图6-12）

要点：虚实分明，穿掌时注意右穿左拉，腰微向左转，对称拧转。

Step forward with the left foot. The toes slightly touch the ground and form a left empty stance. At the same time, change the right fist into a palm and cross it forward from under the right arm, the palm center changing from facing downward to obliquely forward, the palm fingers facing right. Bend the right elbow slightly and lower it down. Withdraw the left fist to the waist, the fist center facing upward. Look at the right palm. (Fig. 6-12)

Key points: Differentiate between "Xu" and "Shi" (Make clear of empty and solid movements). When crossing the bridge, cross with the right palm and pull with the left one. Turn the waist slightly to the left side. The reverse twist action is the same.

图 6-12　左虚步穿桥
Fig. 6-12 Cross "bridge" in a left empty stance

12. 马步冲拳   Thrust fist in a horse stance

左脚向前上半步，脚尖内扣，两腿屈膝半蹲成马步；同时左拳从腰间随转体向左侧冲出，拳眼向上，臂与肩平；右掌随屈肘收至左胸前，掌指向上，掌心向左；目视左拳。（图6-13）

要点：左脚上步、扣脚、转腰变马步时与左冲拳一致，力发于腰。

Make a half-step forward with the left foot, toes facing inward. Bend the knees and do a half squat to form a half horse stance. At the same time, thrust out the left fist to the left side from the waist with the turning of the body, the fist eye facing upward and the arm at shoulder height. Withdraw the right palm to the left side of the chest while bending the elbow, the palm fingers facing upward and the palm center facing left. Lcok at the left fist. (Fig. 6-13)

Key points: Complete the horse stance forming (stepping forward with the left foot, stretching the foot, and turning waist) and the left fist thrusting at the same time. Exert strength from the waist.

图 6-13　马步冲拳
Fig. 6-13 Thrust fist in a horse stance

13. 转身马步劈拳　Straight-arm chop with the body turning in a horse stance

身体向右后转约180°；同时右脚随转体向右后撤步，两腿屈膝成马步；右掌变拳由胸前随转体向右侧劈拳，臂与肩平，拳心向下，力达拳轮；左拳随屈肘收至腰间，拳心向上；目视右拳。（图6-14）

要点：转体时重心落于左腿，以转头转体带动右拳。

Turn the body to the right and move backward for about 180°. At the same time, step backward with the right foot to the right with body turning. Bend knees and form a horse stance. Change the right palm to a fist and make a straight-arm chop from the chest to the right with the turning of the body. Keep the arm at shoulder height, the fist center facing downwards. Convey the strength to "quanlun", i.e. the round hole formed on the side of the little finger. Withdraw the left fist while bending the elbow, the fist center facing upward. Look at the right fist. (Fig. 6-14)

Key points: The center of gravity falls on the left leg when turning the body. Drive the right fist with the turning of head and body.

图6-14　转身马步劈拳
Fig. 6-14 Straight-arm chop with the body turning in a horse stance

14. 回身弓步双推掌

Push palms with the body
turning around in a bow stance

（1）左脚略向里踏步，两腿屈膝，重心偏于右侧成半马步；同时两拳变掌收抱于右腰侧，成蝶掌；目视左侧。［图6-15（1）］

(1) Step slightly inward with the left foot, knees bent, and put the center of gravity slightly on the right side to form a half horse stance. At the same time, change both fists into palms and withdraw them to the right side of the waist, forming the butterfly palm. Look left. [Fig. 6-15(1)]

图 6-15　回身弓步双推掌（1）
Fig. 6-15 Push palms with the body turning around in a bow stance (1)

（2）右脚蹬地，右腿内转挺膝伸直成左弓步；同时腰微左转，两掌向前平推，两臂与肩同高、同宽，翘指坐腕，力达两掌小指侧；目视前方，同时发声"嗨"。［图6-15（2）］

(2) Form a left bow stance after pushing the right foot against the ground and turning the right leg inward before straightening the knee. At the same time, turn the waist slightly to the left, and push both palms straight forward, both arms at shoulder height and shoulder-width apart. Lower the wrists and keep the fingers upright, the strength reaching the little finger sides of both palms. Look straight ahead, and make an utterance of "hi" at the same time. [Fig. 6-15(2)]

图 6-15　回身弓步双推掌（2）
Fig. 6-15　Push palms with the body turning around in a bow stance (2)

要点：半马步为蓄劲，腰微左转；推掌时力起于右脚跟，传于腰，达于手。

Key points: Store up energy when forming the half horse stance. Turn the waist slightly to the left. Exert strength from the right heel when pushing palms. Convey the strength from the waist to hands.

15. 虚步冲拳推掌　　　Thrust fist and push palm in an empty stance

（1）右脚向右前上一步，膝微屈；同时腰微右转，右掌变拳收抱于腰间，拳心向上；左掌弧形摆按至右胸前，掌指向上，掌心向右；目视左掌。［图6-16（1）］

(1) Step forward to the right with the right foot, the knee slightly bent. At the same time, turn the waist slightly right, change the right palm into a fist and withdraw it to the waist, the fist center facing upward. Swing the left palm in an arc shape to the right side of the chest, the palm fingers facing upward, and the palm center facing right. Look at the left palm. [Fig. 6-16(1)]

图 6-16　虚步冲拳推掌（1）
Fig. 6-16 Thrust fist and push palm in an empty stance (1)

（2）左脚向左前方上步，脚尖点地成左虚步；同时腰微左转，右拳、左掌随转体向正前方冲拳、推掌，两臂与肩同高、同宽，右拳心向下，左掌指向上；目视前方。［图6-16（2）］

(2) Step forward to the left with the left foot. The tiptoes slightly touch the ground and form a left empty stance. At the same time, turn the waist slightly to the left, thrust the right fist and push the left palm straight forward with the turning of the body, both arms at shoulder height and shoulder-width apart. The right fist center faces downward, and the left palm fingers face upward. Look straight ahead. [Fig. 6-16(2)]

图 6-16　虚步冲拳推掌（2）
Fig. 6-16 Thrust fist and push palm in an empty stance (2)

要点：虚实分明，手法干脆。

Key points: Differentiate between "Xu" and "Shi" (Make clear of empty and solid movements). Make clear-cut and smooth movements of the hands.

16. 虚步抱拳　　　　　　　Hold fist and palm together in an empty stance

（1）步不动，腰微右转；左掌变拳与右拳随屈肘摆至右胸前，两拳心向下，拳面相对；目视两拳。［图6-17（1）］

（2）两臂外旋，经上向前、向下反臂挂收至腰间，拳心向上；目视正前方。［图6-17（2）］

要点：以腰带臂，眼随手动。

(1) Keep the stance. Turn the waist slightly to right. Turn the left palm into a fist, and swing it together with the right fist to the right side of the chest with the bending of elbows, both fist centers facing downward, and fist surfaces facing each other. Look at both fists. [Fig. 6-17(1)]

(2) Both arms rotate outward, hang upside down on the waist after they move in a up-front-down direction, both fist centers facing upward. Look straight ahead. [Fig. 6-17(2)]

Key points: Use the waist to drive arms. Eyes follow the movement of hands.

图 6-17　虚步抱拳（1）
Fig. 6-17 Hold fist and palm together in an empty stance (1)

图 6-17　虚步抱拳（2）
Fig. 6-17 Hold fist and palm together in an empty stance (2)

收势 {: .float-left} Closing posture

左脚向右脚并步，两腿伸直；同时两拳变掌垂于体侧；目视前方。
（图6-18）

要点：挺膝，夹腿，立腰，提神降气。

Move the left foot to right and form a feet-together stance, keeping both legs straight while changing both fists into palms and placing them on body sides. Look straight ahead. (Fig. 6-18)

Key points: Straighten knees. Squeeze legs together. Keep the waist straight up. Keep spirit up and lower the qi.

图 6-18　收势
Fig. 6-18 Closing posture

二段南拳　　　　　　　　　　Nan Quan: Grade 2

二段南拳
Nan Quan:
Grade 2

动作名称

预备势

第一段

1. 虚步冲拳推掌

2. 虚步抱拳

3. 马步双冲拳

4. 马步挑掌沉桥

5. 马步双推指

6. 马步标掌沉桥

7. 左骑龙步双推掌

8. 右骑龙步双推掌

9. 独立步左蹬脚

10. 跪步推爪

11. 右虚步穿桥

12. 马步侧冲拳

第二段

13. 回身半马步劈桥

14. 左弓步冲拳

15. 独立步右蹬脚

16. 右弓步架桥

17. 左弓步挂盖拳

18. 骑龙步撞拳

19. 虚步切掌

20. 马步撑掌

21. 回身弓步左右抛拳

22. 左弓步抓面爪

23. 虚步冲拳推掌

24. 虚步抱拳

收势

Names of the Movements

Preparatory posture

Section 1

1. Thrust fist and push palm in an empty stance
2. Hold fist and palm together in an empty stance
3. Thrust both fists in a horse stance
4. Stick up palm and sink "bridge" in a horse stance
5. Double-finger-pushing in a horse stance
6. Thrust palms forward and sink "bridge" in a horse stance
7. Push palms in a left dragon-riding stance
8. Push palms in a right dragon-riding stance
9. Kick with the left heel on a single foot
10. Push claw in a kneeling stance
11. Cross "bridge" in a right empty stance
12. Side fist thrust in a horse stance

Section 2

13. Chop "bridge" with the body turning around in a half horse stance
14. Thrust fist in a left bow stance
15. Kick with the right heel on a single foot
16. Build "bridge" in a right bow stance
17. Guagaiquan (Fists swing overhead) in a left bow stance
18. Zhuangquan (Bump fist) in a dragon-riding stance
19. Palm cutting in an empty stance
20. Hold up palm in a horse stance
21. Throw fist left and right with the body turning around in a bow stance
22. Scratch-face claw in a left bow stance
23. Thrust fist and push palm in an empty stance
24. Hold fist and palm together in an empty stance

Closing posture

预备势   Preparatory posture

（1）两脚并步，直腿站立；直臂，两掌贴靠于两腿外侧；目视前方。［图6-19（1）］

（2）两腿不动，两掌变拳提抱于腰间，拳心向上；目视前方。［图6-19（2）］

要点：挺膝，收腹，敛臀，立腰，提神降气。

(1) Stand with both feet together with straight legs. Place both palms against the outside of the two legs, arms straight. Look straight ahead. [Fig. 6-19(1)]

(2) Keep the legs still. Change palms into fists and withdraw them to the waist, the fist centers facing upward. Look straight ahead. [Fig. 6-19(2)]

Key points: Straighten knees. Squeeze legs togeher. Draw in belly, hold back buttocks, and keep the waist straight up. Keep spirits up and lower the qi.

图 6-19　预备势（1）　　　　　图 6-19　预备势（2）
Fig. 6-19 Preparatory posture (1)　　Fig. 6-19 Preparatory posture (2)

第一段　Section 1

1. 虚步冲拳推掌　　　　Thrust fist and push palm in an empty stance

（1）右脚向右前上步，脚尖外展，膝微屈；同时腰微右转，右拳提至右胸前，拳心向下；左拳变掌弧形向上摆至右胸前，掌指向上，掌心与右拳面相对；目视右拳。［图6-20（1）］

（2）左脚向前上半步，脚尖点地成左虚步；同时腰微左转，右拳与左掌向前冲拳、推掌，两臂伸直与肩同高、同宽，左掌心与右拳面均向前；目视前方。［图6-20（2）］

要点：右脚与左脚上步时重心下沉，虚实分明，冲拳、推掌发力于腰，眼随手动。

(1) Step forward to the right with the right foot, toes turning out and the knee slightly bent. At the same time, turn the waist slightly right, and lift the right fist to the right side of the chest, the fist center facing downward. Change the left fist into a palm and swing it in an arc shape to the right side of the chest, the palm fingers facing upward, and the palm center facing the right fist surface. Look at the right fist. [Fig. 6-20(1)]

(2) Make a half-step forward with the left foot. The tiptoes slightly touch the ground and form a left empty stance. At the same time, turn the waist slightly to the left, thrust the right fist and push the left palm forward. Straighten both arms at shoulder height and shoulder-width apart. Both the left palm center and the right fist surface face forward. Look straight ahead. [Fig. 6-20(2)]

Key points: When stepping with the right and left foot, lower the center of gravity. Differentiate between "Xu" and "Shi" (Make clear of empty and solid movements). Exert strength when thrusting the fist and pushing the palm. Eyes follow the movement of hands.

图6-20 虚步冲拳推掌（1）

Fig. 6-20 Thrust fist and push palm in an empty stance (1)

图6-20 虚步冲拳推掌（2）

Fig. 6-20 Thrust fist and push palm in an empty stance (2)

2.虚步抱拳　　　　　　　　Hold fist and palm together in an empty stance

（1）步不动，腰微右转；同时左掌变拳，两拳随屈肘拉至右侧胸前，拳面相对；目视两拳。［图6-21（1）］

（2）步仍不动，腰微左转；同时两臂外旋，两拳经上向前反臂挂收于腰间，拳心向上；目视前方。［图6-21（2）］

要点：虚步稳固，以腰带臂。

(1) Keep the stance. Turn the waist slightly to the right. At the same time, change the left palm into a fist. Pull the two fists to the right side of the chest while bending elbows, the fist surfaces facing each other. Look at both fists. [Fig. 6-21(1)]

(2) Still keep the stance. Turn the waist slightly to the left. Rotate both arms ourward, and then hang both fists upside down on the waist after moving them in an up-front direction, the fist centers facing upward. Look straight ahead. [Fig. 6-21(2)]

Key points: Keep the empty stance stable. Use the waist to drive arms.

图 6-21　虚步抱拳（1）
Fig. 6-21 Hold fist and palm together in an empty stance (1)

图 6-21　虚步抱拳（2）
Fig. 6-21 Hold fist and palm together in an empty stance (2)

3. 马步双冲拳　　　　　　　　　　　Thrust both fists in a horse stance

（1）右腿微屈膝支撑身体，左脚由前经右脚内侧弧形向左开步；两腿屈膝半蹲；目视前方。［图6-22（1）］

（2）身体重心移至左腿；右脚由右侧经左脚内侧向前再向右侧弧形开步，两腿屈膝半蹲成马步；目视前方。［图6-22（2）］

（3）马步不动；两拳直线向前冲出，拳心向下，两臂与肩同高、同宽；目视前方，同时发声"嗨"。［图6-22（3）］

要点：左、右脚向左、右开步时要重心平稳，全脚掌贴地，弧形开步；冲拳时腰先微左（或右）转，以腰发力为主。

(1) Bend the right leg slightly to support the body, and step to the left with the left foot in an arc shape in a forward-left direction through the inner side of the right foot. Bend knees to do a half squat. Look left. [Fig. 6-22(1)]

(2) Shift the weight to the left leg. Step to the right with the right foot in an arc shape in a forward-right direction through the inner side of the left foot. Bend knees to do a half squat. Look straight ahead. [Fig. 6-22(2)]

(3) Keep the horse stance, and thrust both fists straight forward, both fist centers facing down, and both arms at shoulder height and shoulder-width apart. Look straight ahead, and make an utterance of "hi" at the same time. [Fig. 6-22(3)]

Key points: Keep the center of gravity stable when the left or right foot moves to the left or the right. Keep the soles of both feet on the ground. Step in an arc shape. Turn the waist slightly to the left (or the right) before thrusting fists, and exert strength mainly from the waist.

图 6-22　马步双冲拳（1）
Fig. 6-22 Thrust both fists in a horse stance (1)

图 6-22　马步双冲拳（2）
Fig. 6-22 Thrust both fists in a horse stance (2)

图 6-22　马步双冲拳（3）
Fig. 6-22 Thrust both fists in a horse stance (3)

4. 马步挑掌沉桥　　　Stick up palm and sink "bridge" in a horse stance

（1）马步不动；两拳变掌随屈臂经下向里分挑至两肩前，沉肩垂肘，两掌心向里，掌指向上；目视前方。［图6-23（1）］

(1) Keep the horse stance. Change both fists into palms and lift them inward in a bottom-up direction to the front of shoulders with the bending of arms. Lower shoulders and elbows, with both palm centers facing inward and palm fingers facing upward. Look straight ahead. [Fig. 6-23(1)]

图 6-23　马步挑掌沉桥（1）
Fig. 6-23 Stick up palm and sink "bridge" in a horse stance (1)

（2）马步仍不动；两前臂内旋下沉与腹部同高，两掌心向下，掌指微外展；目视两掌。［图6-23（2）］

(2) Still keep the horse stance. Rotate both forearms inward and lower them to the height of the belly, both palms facing down and palm fingers turning slightly outward. Look at both palms. [Fig. 6-23(2)]

图 6-23　马步挑掌沉桥（2）
Fig. 6-23 Stick up palm and sink "bridge" in a horse stance (2)

要点：马步沉稳，挑掌和沉桥均以肘关节为轴，夹腋沉肘，动作幅度宜小。

Key points: Keep the horse stance stable. Take the elbow joint as the axis when sticking up palms and sinking "bridge" (arms), armpits clamped, and elbows lowered. Keep the range of movements small.

5. 马步双推指　　　　　　　　Double-finger-pushing in a horse stance

（1）两掌变单指手收至腰间，掌心向下；目视左下方。［图6-24（1）］

（2）两臂极度紧张用力，两指慢慢向前推出，翘指坐腕，掌心向前，两臂与肩同高、同宽；目视前方。［图6-24（2）］

要点：马步沉稳，两臂刚劲有力。

(1) Change both palms into the single-finger position and withdraw them to the waist, palm centers facing down. Look left. [Fig. 6-24(1)]

(2) Exert extreme strength with both arms. Push the two fingers lowly forward. Lower the wrists and keep the two fingers upright. Both palm centers face forward, and both arms are at shoulder height and shoulder-width apart. Look straight ahead. [Fig. 6-24(2)]

Key points: Keep the horse stance stable. Be strong and forceful with the arms.

图 6-24　马步双推指（1）
Fig. 6-24 Double-finger-pushing in a horse stance (1)

图 6-24　马步双推指（2）
Fig. 6-24 Double-finger-pushing in a horse stance (2)

6. 马步标掌沉桥　　Thrust palms forward and sink "bridge" in a horse stance

（1）马步不动；两臂屈肘，两指挑至肩上，掌心斜向里，两肘正对前方；目视右肘。［图6-25（1）］

（2）两肘下沉，两指收至腰间，掌心向里；目视左侧。［图6-25（2）］

(1) Stay in a horse stance. Bend the elbows, and lift the two fingers to the shoulders, with palm centers facing obliquely inward, and elbows facing forward. Look at the right elbow. [Fig. 6-25(1)]

(2) Lower the elbows. Draw the two fingers back to the waist, with palm centers facing inward. Look left. [Fig. 6-25(2)]

图 6-25　马步标掌沉桥（1）
Fig. 6-25 Thrust palms forward
and sink "bridge" in a horse
stance (1)

图 6-25　马步标掌沉桥（2）
Fig. 6-25 Thrust palms forward
and sink "bridge" in a horse
stance (2)

（3）两指变掌快速向前标出，拇指向上，掌心相对，两臂与肩同高、同宽；目视两掌。［图6-25（3）］

（4）两前臂快速下沉，垂肘翘指；目视前方。［图6-25（4）］

(3) Change back to palms from the single-finger position and thrust them forward quickly, with thumbs facing upward, palm centers facing each other, and arms at shoulder height and shoulder-width apart. Look at both palms. [Fig. 6-25(3)]

(4) Make the forearms sink quickly, lower elbows and keep fingers upright. Look straight ahead. [Fig. 6-25(4)]

图 6-25 马步标掌沉桥（3）
Fig. 6-25 Thrust palms forward and sink "bridge" in a horse stance(3)

图 6-25 马步标掌沉桥（4）
Fig. 6-25 Thrust palms forward and sink "bridge" in a horse stance(4)

要点：连续4个分解动作，马步均保持沉稳，上体勿前倾后仰；标掌要快速有爆发劲；沉桥时用劲短促，力达前臂尺骨侧。

Key points: For the four consecutive movement segments, keep the horse stance stable, and do not lean forward or backward. Be quick and explosive at palm thrusting. Make "jin" (strength) short when sinking the "bridge". Convey the strength to the ulnar side of the forearms.

7. 左骑龙步双推掌   *Push palms in a left dragon-riding stance*

（1）左脚向左前方上步，脚尖向左；两腿屈膝半蹲，重心偏于右腿成半马步；同时腰微右转，两掌随屈肘收抱于右侧成蝶掌；目视左侧。[图6-26（1）]

（2）右脚内转并略向前跟进，屈膝下沉成左骑龙步；同时腰微左转，两掌向左前方下推，两臂微屈；左掌心向下，右掌心向上，掌指均向右，小指侧成一横线，高与胸平；目视两掌。[图6-26（2）]

要点：半马步蓄劲，腰微右转；双推掌时，左臂成半圆，右肘下沉，发力于腰。

(1) Step forward to the left with the left foot, toes facing left. Bend knees, do a half squat, and shift weight on the right leg to form a half horse stance. At the same time, turn the waist slightly right, draw back both palms to the right side, and form the butterfly palm with the bending of elbows. Look left. [Fig. 6-26(1)]

(2) Turn the right foot inward and step slightly forward, bend and lower the knees to form a left dragon-riding stance. At the same time, turn the waist slightly left, push both palms down to the left front, and bend the elbows slightly. The left palm faces down, the right palm faces up, and the palm fingers all face to the right, with the little finger sides forming a horizontal line at chest height. Look at both palms. [Fig. 6-26(2)]

Key points: Store up energy when forming the half horse stance. Turn the waist slightly to the right. When pushing palms, the left arm is formed into a semicircle, the right elbow is lowered, and the strength is exerted from the waist.

图6-26　左骑龙步双推掌（1）
Fig. 6-26　Push palms in a left
dragon-riding stance (1)

图6-26　左骑龙步双推掌（2）
Fig. 6-26　Push palms in a left
dragon-riding stance (2)

8. 右骑龙步双推掌　　　　Push palms in a right dragon-riding stance

（1）右脚向右前方上步，脚尖向右，两腿屈膝半蹲，重心偏于左腿成半马步；同时腰微左转，两掌随屈肘收抱于左侧成蝶掌；目视右侧。［图6-27（1）］

（2）左脚内转并略向前跟进，屈膝下沉成右骑龙步；同时腰微右转，两掌向右前方平推，两肘微屈；右掌心向下，左掌心向上，掌指均向左，小指侧成一横线，高与胸平；目视两掌。［图6-27（2）］

要点：半马步蓄劲，腰微左转；双推掌时，右臂成半圆，左肘下沉，发力于腰。

(1) Step forward to the right with the right foot, toes facing right. Bend knees, do a half squat, and shift weight on the left leg to form a half horse stance. At the same time, turn the waist slightly left, draw back both palms to the left side, and form the butterfly palm with the bending of elbows. Look right. [Fig. 6-27(1)]

(2) Turn the left foot inward and step slightly forward, bend and lower the knees to form a right dragon-riding stance. At the same time, turn the waist slightly right, push both palms down to the right front, and bend the elbows slightly. The right palm faces down, the left palm faces up, and the palm fingers all face to the left, with the little

finger sides forming a horizontal line at chest height. Look at both palms. [Fig. 6-27(2)]

Key points: Store up energy when forming the half horse stance. Turn the waist slightly to the left. When pushing palms, the right arm is formed into a semicircle, the left elbow is lowered, and the strength is exerted from the waist.

图 6-27　右骑龙步双推掌（1）
Fig. 6-27 Push palms in a right
dragon-riding stance (1)

图 6-27　右骑龙步双推掌（2）
Fig. 6-27 Push palms in a right
dragon-riding stances (2)

9. 独立步左蹬脚　　　　　　　　　　Kick with the left heel on a single foot

（1）右脚向里活步，右腿屈膝，左脚跟离地；同时腰微左转，两掌变虎爪经头上交叉（左手在外）后摆至两侧，手心向外，腕与肩同高；目视前方。［图6-28（1）］

（2）右腿伸直独立支撑，左腿屈膝抬起，以脚跟为力点向前蹬出，挺膝勾脚，腿高于胯；目视前方。［图6-28（2）］

要点：支撑腿挺膝收髋，五趾抓地；蹬脚屈伸明显，发力快脆。

(1) Make a moving step inward with the right foot. Bend the right knee and keep the left heel off the ground. At the same time, turn the waist slightly to the left, change palms into tiger claws, cross them over head (with the left hand outside), and then swing them to the sides, with claw centers facing outward and wrists at shoulder height. Look straight ahead. [Fig. 6-28(1)]

(2) Keep the right leg straight for independent support. Bend and raise the left leg. And then kick with heel forward, exerting strength from the heel, keeping the knee straight, and turning the toes upwards, the leg higher than hips. Look straight ahead. [Fig. 6-28(2)]

Key points: Keep the supporting leg and the knee straight, retracting hips and grabbing the ground with the five toes. Make the flexion and extension of the kick obvious. Exert strength in a fast and smooth way.

图 6-28　独立步左蹬脚（1）
Fig. 6-28 Kick with the left heel on a single foot (1)

图 6-28　独立步左蹬脚（2）
Fig. 6-28 Kick with the left heel on a single foot (2)

10. 跪步推爪   Push claw in a kneeling stance

（1）左脚向前落步，两腿屈膝，重心偏于右腿成半马步；同时腰微右转，右虎爪收至腰间，手心向下；左虎爪由左侧弧形摆按至体前，手心向前，臂与肩平；目视左前方。［图6-29（1）］

（2）右腿向前跟进半步，两腿屈膝下蹲成跪步；同时右虎爪直线向前推出，臂与肩平，手心向前；左虎爪收至右肘下内侧，手心斜向右；目视右虎爪。［图6-29（2）］

要点：左脚落步与左虎爪下按一致，推右虎爪时发力于腰。

(1) Step forward with the left foot, bend knees, and put more weight on the right leg to form a half horse stance. At the same time, turn the waist slightly to the right, and withdraw the right tiger claw to the waist, the claw center facing downward. Swing the left tiger claw from left to front in an arc shape, with the claw center facing forward and the arm at shoulder height. Look forward to the left. [Fig. 6-29(1)]

(2) Make a half-step forward with the right leg, bend knees and do a squat to form a kneeling stance. At the same time, push the right tiger claw straight ahead, with the arm at shoulder height and claw center facing forward. Withdraw the left tiger claw to the inner side of the right elbow, the claw center facing right. Look at the right tiger claw. [Fig. 6-29(2)]

Key points: The stepping of the left foot should be done simultaneously with the pressing of the left tiger claw. The strength should be exerted from the waist when pushing the right claw.

图 6-29　跪步推爪（1）　　　　　图 6-29　跪步推爪（2）
Fig. 6-29 Push claw in a kneeling stance (1)　　Fig. 6-29 Push claw in a kneeling stance (2)

11. 右虚步穿桥　　　　　　　Cross "bridge" in a right empty stance

右脚向前上步，脚尖点地成右虚步；同时右虎爪变拳，拳心向上；左虎爪变掌，掌心向下沿右臂向前穿出后变掌心向前；右拳收至腰间，拳心向上；目视左掌。（图6-30）

要点：穿桥时左臂先内旋后外旋，腰先微左转后右转，拧腰旋臂。

Step forward with the right foot, tiptoes slightly touching the ground, and form a right empty stance. At the same time, change the right tiger claw to a fist, with the fist center facing upward. Change the left tiger claw to a palm with the palm center facing down, and cross it forward from under the arm, with the palm center facing forward. Withdraw the right fist back to the waist, the fist center facing upward. Look at the left palm. (Fig. 6-30)

Key points: When crossing the bridge, rotate the left arm inward first and then outward, and turn the waist first slightly to the left and then to the right. Twist the waist and rotate arms.

图 6-30　右虚步穿桥
Fig. 6-30 Cross "bridge" in a right empty stance

12. 马步侧冲拳　　　　　　　　　　　　Side fist thrust in a horse stance

右脚向前上半步，脚尖内扣，两腿屈膝半蹲成马步；同时身体向左转约90°，右拳随体转向右侧冲出，拳眼向上，臂与肩平；左掌随屈肘收至右胸前，掌心向右，掌指向上；目视右拳。（图6-31）

要点：右脚向前上步与转体和冲拳要一致，冲拳时发力于腰。

Make a half-step forward with the right leg, toes facing inward. Bend knees and do a half squat to form a horse stance. At the same time, thrust the right fist to the right side while turning the waist to the left at a 90-degree angle, with the fist eye facing upward and arm at shoulder height. Withdraw the left palm to the right side of the chest with the bending of the elbow, with the palm center facing right and palm fingers facing upward. Look at the right fist. (Fig. 6-31)

Key points: Step forward with the right foot and thrust the fist while turning the body at the same time. Exert strength from the waist when thrusting.

图 6-31　马步侧冲拳
Fig. 6-31 Side fist thrust in a horse stance

第二段 Section 2

13. 回身半马步劈桥
Chop "bridge" with the body turning around in a half horse stance

左脚向左侧稍活步变脚尖向左，两腿屈膝，重心偏于右腿成半马步；同时腰微左转，左掌变拳，左臂内旋以前臂尺骨侧（小指侧）为力点向左斜下方劈出，左拳心向下；右拳收回腰间，拳心向上；目视左拳。（图6-32）

要点：回身活步时，重心控制在右侧，沉重稳固。

Make a small moving step to the left with the left foot, toes facing left. Bend knees, put more weight on the right leg and form a half horse stance. At the same time, turn the waist slightly to the left, change the left palm into a fist, rotate the left arm inward, and chop it down to the left by exerting strength from the ulnar side of the forearm (the side of the little finger), with the left fist center facing downward. Draw the right fist back to waist, with the fist center facing upward. Look at the left fist. (Fig. 6-32)

Key points: When turning the body and making a moving step, keep the center of gravity on the right side in a solid and stable way.

图 6-32　回身半马步劈桥
Fig. 6-32 Chop "bridge" with the body turning around in a half horse stance

14. 左弓步冲拳　　　　　　　　　Thrust fist in a left bow stance

右脚蹬地，右腿内转挺膝伸直成左弓步；同时右拳向前冲出，拳心向下，臂与肩平；左拳收回腰间，拳心向上；目视右拳。（图6-33）

要点：冲拳要充分借助于蹬地、扣膝、转胯、转腰的力量。

Form a left bow stance after pushing the right foot against the ground and turning the right leg inward before straightening the knee. At the same time, thrust the right fist forward, the fist eye facing down and the arm at shoulder height. Withdraw the left fist to the waist, the fist center facing upward. Look at the right fist. (Fig. 6-33)

Key points: When thrusting, make full use of the strength exerted from pushing and turning the right leg, twisting the knee, turning the hips and the waist.

图 6-33　左弓步冲拳
Fig. 6-33 Thrust fist in a left bow stance

15. 独立步右蹬脚　　　　　　　　Kick with the right heel on a single foot

（1）左脚稍向内活步，全脚掌贴地，右脚跟离地稍向前跟进，两膝微屈；同时两拳变虎爪，左虎爪从右臂下穿出后与右虎爪分摆至两侧，手心向外，臂与肩平；目视前方。［图6-34（1）］

（2）左腿直立支撑，右腿屈膝上抬后再向前蹬出，挺膝勾脚，力达脚跟；目视前方。［图6-34（2）］

要点：屈伸明显，发力快脆。

(1) Make a small moving step inward with the left foot, with the sole on the ground. Lift the right heel off the ground and step slightly forward, bending both knees slightly. At the same time, change both fists into tiger claws, make the left one cross forward from under the right arm, and then swing it together with the right claw to the sides, with both claw centers facing outward and arms at shoulder height. Look straight ahead. [Fig. 6-34(1)]

(2) Keep the left leg straight for support. Bend and raise the right leg, and then kick with heel forward, keeping the knee straight and turning the toes upward. Convey strength to the heel. Look straight ahead. [Fig. 6-34(2)]

Key points: Make the flexion and extension of the kick obvious. Exert strength in a fast and smooth way.

图 6-34　独立步右蹬脚（1）
Fig. 6-34 Kick with the right heel on a single foot (1)

图 6-34　独立步右蹬脚（2）
Fig. 6-34 Kick with the right heel on a single foot (2)

16. 右弓步架桥　　　　　　　　Build "bridge" in a right bow stance

（1）右脚落地，两腿微向右，重心偏于右腿成半马步；同时腰微左转，两虎爪变掌回收至左腰侧，右上左下，掌心均向上；目视右掌。［图6-35（1）］

（2）左脚蹬地，左腿内转挺膝伸直成右弓步；同时腰微右转，两掌经上分架于头的斜上方，掌心斜向上，臂呈弧形；目视前方。［图6-35（2）］

要点：右脚落步稍偏右斜前方，半马步时转腰蓄劲，架桥时发力于左腿的蹬转。

(1) Land the right foot. Both legs face slightly to the right side, and put more weight on the right leg to form a half horse stance. At the same time, turn the waist slightly to the left, change both tiger claws to palms and withdraw them to the left side of the waist, with the right one on the top and the left one on the bottom, both palms facing upward. Look at the right palm. [Fig. 6-35(1)]

(2) Push the left foot against the ground. Turn the left leg inward and straighten the knee into a right bow stance. At the same time, turn the waist slightly to the right, place the palms obliquely above the head, with the palm centers facing upward, and arms in arc shape. Look straight ahead. [Fig. 6-35(2)]

Key points: When making a landing step with the right foot, move it forward slightly to the right. Store up energy when twisting the waist to form a half horse stance. Exert strength from pulling and turning the left leg when building the "bridge".

图 6-35　右弓步架桥（1）　　　　图 6-35　右弓步架桥（2）
Fig. 6-35 Build "bridge" in a right bow stance (1)　　Fig. 6-35 Build "bridge" in a right bow stance (2)

17. 左弓步挂盖拳 Guagaiquan (Fists swing overhead) in a left bow stance

（1）左脚向前上步，脚尖向左，两腿屈膝；同时腰微右转，两掌变拳，右拳直臂经下摆至右侧斜下方，拳心向下；左臂内旋，左拳经下挂至体前，拳心斜向下；目视右拳。［图6-36（1）］

（2）右脚尖内扣，右腿内转挺膝伸直成左弓步；同时腰微左转，右拳经上盖至体前下方，拳心斜向内；左拳随臂外旋经上向下反挂至左后侧，拳心斜向下；目视前方。［图6-36（2）］

要点：左脚上步时微向右转腰，挂盖拳以腰带臂；完成弓步盖拳时，四肢对称用力，重心平稳。

(1) Step forward with the left foot, toes facing left. Bend both knees. At the same time, turn the waist slightly to the right, change both palms into fists, and swing the right fist from below to the obliquely downside of the right, with the arm straight and the fist center facing down. Rotate the left arm inward, and hang it to the front from downside, with the fist center facing obliquely down. Look at the right fist. [Fig. 6-36(1)]

(2) Toes of the right foot face inward. Form a left bow stance after pushing the right foot against the ground and turning the right leg inward before straightening the knee. At the same time, turn the waist slightly to the left, thump the right fist from the upper body to the front lower side, the fist center facing obliquely inward. The left fist follows the external rotation of the arm in a top-down direction, and then hangs upside down on the left back side, with the fist center facing obliquely downward. Look straight ahead. [Fig. 6-36(2)]

Key points: When stepping forward with the left foot, turn the waist slightly to the right, and use the waist to drive arms in guagaiquan. When completing gaiquan in a bow stance, exert symmetrical strength on the limbs, and keep the center of gravity steady.

图 6-36　左弓步挂盖拳（1）
Fig. 6-36 Guagaiquan (Fists swing overhead) in a left bow stance (1)

图 6-36　左弓步挂盖拳（2）
Fig. 6-36 Guagaiquan (Fists swing overhead) in a left bow stance (2)

18. 骑龙步撞拳　　　Zhuangquan (Bump fist) in a dragon-riding stance

右脚向前上步，屈膝半蹲，左腿屈膝下跪成骑龙步；同时，右拳向上、向后经下向前上弧形撞至体前，拳心向里，拳面向上，与肩同高；左拳变掌由后向下摆至体前，附于右前臂；目视右拳。（图6-37）

要点：右拳先动，弧形抄撞；上步与撞拳一致，眼随右拳环视。

Step forward with the right foot, bend the knee and do a half squat. Bend the left leg and kneel down into a dragon-riding stance. At the same time, make a bumping strike with the right fist to the front of the body in an arc shape after moving it in a upwar-backward-forwrd direction, with the fist center facing inward and the fist surface facing upward at shoulder height. Change the left fist into a palm, and then swing it from the back to the front of the body, attaching to the right forearm. Look at the right fist. (Fig. 6-37)

Key points: Move the right fist first, and then bump it in an arc in the twinkling of an eye. Stepping forward and bumping fist should be well coordinated, and the eyes follow the right fist to look around.

图 6-37 骑龙步撞拳
Fig. 6-37 Zhuangquan (Bump fist) in a dragon-riding stance

19. 虚步切掌   Palm cutting in an empty stance

身体重心后移，右脚向后撤回半步，脚尖点地成右虚步；同时左掌沿右前臂向前横掌切出，掌指向右，掌心斜向前下方；右拳变掌随右臂内旋拉回至右胸前，掌心向下；目视左掌。（图6-38）

要点：右脚回收，腰微右转，右拳变掌回拉与左掌前切用力方向相反，动作协调一致。

Move the center of gravity backward, make a half step back with the right foot with toes slightly touching the ground, and form a right empty stance. At the same time, the left palm cuts forward horizontally along the right forearm, with the palm fingers facing right and the palm center facing obliquely down. Turn the right fist into a palm and pull it back to the right side of the chest with the inward rotation of the right arm, the palm facing downward. Look at the left palm. (Fig. 6-38)

Key points: Withdraw the right foot. Slightly turn the waist to the right. The direction of pulling the right palm (changed from the fist) is opposite to that of cutting forward with the left palm. The movements should be well coordinated.

图 6-38　虚步切掌

Fig. 6-38 Palm cutting in an empty stance

20. 马步撑掌　　　　　　　　　　　　　　　Hold up palm in a horse stance

　　右脚向前上半步，脚尖内扣，两腿屈膝半蹲成马步；同时腰左转约90°，右掌随转体向右侧斜下横掌切出，掌心斜向下；左掌回收至右肩前，掌心向右；目视右掌。（图6-39）

　　要点：切掌时右臂内旋，发力于腰。

Make a half-step forward with the right foot, toes facing inward. Bend knees and do a half squat to form a horse stance. At the same time, thrust the right palm down to the right side when turning the waist to the left for about 90°. Make a cutting strike with the right palm obliquely downward while turning the body, with the palm center facing obliquely down. Withdraw the left palm to the right shoulder, with the palm center facing right. Look at the right fist. (Fig. 6-39)

Key points: The right arm rotates inward when the palm cuts. Exert strength from the waist.

图 6-39　马步撑掌

Fig. 6-39 Hold up palm in a horse stance

21. 回身弓步左右抛拳   Throw fist left and right with the body turning around in a bow stance

（1）上体稍向左转；同时两掌变拳，拳心斜向下；目视右拳。动作不停，左脚向左后活步，左腿屈膝，右腿内转稍向前跟进后挺膝成左弓步；同时腰微左转，右拳由右侧随转体向右上抛起，拳眼向后；左拳经下挂摆至左后侧举，拳心向下；目视前方。［图6-40（1）］

（2）右脚向右侧稍活步，右腿屈膝，左腿内转稍向前跟进后挺膝成右弓步；同时腰微右转，左拳由左侧随转体向左上抛起，拳眼向前；右拳由后经下挂摆至右后侧举，拳心向下；目视前方。［图6-40（2）］

要点：回身左右抛拳时步幅移动不宜太大，稍作左右活步即可；上肢动作幅度宜大，注重以腰带臂，左右拧转对称用力。

(1) Turn the upper body slightly left while changing both palms into fists, with fist centers facing obliquely downward. Look at the right fist. Keep smooth movements. Make a moving step backward to the left with the left foot. Form a left bow stance after turning the right leg inward, stepping it forward, and keeping the knee straight. At the same time, turn the waist slightly left, and throw the right fist up from the right side with the body turning, the fist eye facing backward. Swing the left fist from below to the right back side with a side lift, the fist eye facing downward. Look straight ahead. [Fig. 6-40(1)]

(2) Make a small moving step to the right with the right foot. Bend the right knee. Form a right bow stance after turning the left leg inward, stepping it forward, and keeping the knee straight. At the same time, turn the waist slightly right, and throw the left fist up from the left side with the body turning, the fist eye facing backward. Swing the right fist from below to the right back side with a side lift, the fist eye facing downward. Look straight ahead. [Fig. 6-40(2)]

Key points: When throwing the fist left and right with the turning of the body, do not make a big stride. Just have a moving step. Use the waist to drive arms with a large range of movements of the upper body. Exert symmetrical strength when twisting left and right.

图 6-40　回身弓步左右抛拳（1）
Fig. 6-40 Throw fist left and right with the body turning around in a bow stance (1)

图 6-40　回身弓步左右抛拳（2）
Fig. 6-40 Throw fist left and right with the body turning around in a bow stance (2)

22. 左弓步抓面爪　　　　　Scratch-face claw in a left bow stance

（1）左脚向左侧上步，脚尖向左，两腿屈膝，重心偏于右侧成半马步；同时两拳变虎爪，右虎爪收于腰间，手心向上；左虎爪由上扣按至左侧，手心斜向下；目视左侧。［图6-41（1）］

（2）右腿内转，挺膝伸直成左弓步；同时右虎爪由腰间向前直抓，手与面同高，手心向前；左虎爪回收至右肘内侧下方，手心向右；目视前方，同时发声"嗨"。［图6-41（2）］

要点：半马步闭气蓄劲，腰微右转，意在左虎爪的扣按（防守之意）；右虎爪前抓时注重右腿的蹬转，力起于根。

(1) Step to the left with the left foot, toes facing left. Bend both knees. Put more weight on the right leg and then form a half horse stance. At the same time, change both fists into tiger claws and withdraw the right one to the waist, the claw center facing upward. Press the left tiger claw from the top to the left side, the claw center facing obliquely downward. Look left. [Fig. 6-41(1)]

(2) Turn the right leg inward and straighten the knee to form a left bow stance. At the same time, the right tiger claw scratches straight ahead from the waist, with the claw at face height and the hand center facing forward. Withdraw the left tiger claw under the inner side of the right elbow, with the claw center facing right. Look straight ahead, and make an utterance of "hi" at the same time. [Fig. 6-41(2)]

Key points: Hold breath to store up energy, and turn the waist slightly to the right in order to press the left tiger claw (for defense). Push and turn the right leg when the right claw scratches, with the strength from the root, i.e. feet.

图 6-41　左弓步抓面爪（1）　　　　图 6-41　左弓步抓面爪（2）
Fig. 6-41 Scratch-face claw in a left bow stance (1)　　Fig. 6-41 Scratch-face claw in a left bow stance (2)

23. 虚步冲拳推掌　　　　Thrust fist and push palm in an empty stance

（1）右脚向右前上一小步，膝微屈；同时腰微右转，右虎爪变拳收至腰间，拳心向上；左虎爪变掌弧形经上摆按至右胸前，掌心向右，掌指向上；目视左掌。［图6-42（1）］

（2）左脚向左前上步，脚尖点地成左虚步；同时腰微左转，右拳、左掌随转体向正前方冲拳、推掌，两臂与肩同高、同宽，右拳面与左掌心向前；目视前方。［图6-42（2）］

要点：虚实分明，手法干脆。

(1) Make a little step forward to the right with the right foot. Bend knees slightly. At the same time, turn the waist slightly to the right, and change the right tiger claw into a fist before withdrawing it to the waist, with the fist center facing upward. Change the left tiger claw into a palm and press it in an arc shape to the right side of the chest, with the palm center facing right and palm fingers facing upward. Look at the left palm. [Fig. 6-42(1)]

(2) Step forward to the left with the left leg. The tiptoes slightly touch the ground and form a left empty stance. At the same time, turn the waist slightly to the left, thrust the right fist and push the left palm forward with the turning of the body, both arms at shoulder height and shoulder-width apart. The right fist surface and the left palm center face forward. Look straight ahead. [Fig. 6-42(2)]

Key points: Differentiate between "Xu" and "Shi" (Make clear of empty and solid movements). Make clear-cut and smooth movements of the hands.

图 6-42　虚步冲拳推掌（1）
Fig. 6-42 Thrust fist and push palm and in an empty stance (1)

图 6-42　虚步冲拳推掌（2）
Fig. 6-42 Thrust fist and push palm and in an empty stance (2)

24. 虚步抱拳　　　　　　　Hold fist and palm together in an empty stance

（1）步不动，腰微右转；左掌变拳与右拳随屈肘摆至右胸前，两拳心向下，拳面相对；目视两拳。［图6-43（1）］

（2）两臂外旋，两拳经上向前向下反臂挂收至腰间，拳心向上；目视正前方。［图6-43（2）］

要点：以腰带臂，眼随手动。

(1) Keep the stance. Turn the waist slightly to the right. Change the left palm into a fist, and then swing both fists to the right side of the chest, the fist surfaces facing downward. Look at both fists. [Fig. 6-43(1)]

(2) Rotate both arms outward, and then hang both fists upside down on the waist after moving them in an up-front direction, the palm centers facing upward. Look straight ahead. [Fig. 6-43(2)]

Key points: Use the waist to drive arms. Eyes follow the movement of hands.

图 6-43　虚步抱拳（1）
Fig. 6-43 Hold fist and palm together in an empty stance (1)

图 6-43　虚步抱拳（2）
Fig. 6-43 Hold fist and palm together in an empty stance (2)

收势   Closing posture

左脚向右脚并步，两腿伸直；同时两拳变掌垂于体侧；目视前方。
（图6-44）

要点：挺膝，夹腿，立腰，提神降气。

Move the left foot to right and form a feet-together stance, keeping both legs straight while changing both fists into palms and placing them on body sides. Look straight ahead. (Fig. 6-44)

Key points: Straighten knees. Squeeze legs together. Keep the waist straight up. Keep spirit up and lower the qi.

图 6-44　收势
Fig. 6-44 Closing posture

三段南拳 Nan Quan: Grade 3

三段南拳
Nan Quan:
Grade 3

动作名称

预备势

第一段

1. 虚步冲拳推掌

2. 并步抱拳

3. 左弓步侧冲拳

4. 左弓步截桥

5. 弓步圈桥标掌

6. 马步连环掌

7. 马步双推指

8. 马步标掌沉桥

9. 并步抱拳

10. 左蹬脚

11. 独立步推指

12. 跪步盖拳

13. 右弓步架桥

14. 回身挂盖拳

15. 退步格打

16. 右弓步侧冲拳

第二段

17. 勒手左踩腿

18. 骑龙步双推掌

19. 单蝶步劈桥

20. 右弓步架打

21. 弓步左右抛拳

22. 左弓步侧冲拳

23. 虚步鹤嘴手

24. 分掌弹踢

25. 分步撑掌

26. 骑龙步双推掌

27. 麒麟步左弓步蝶掌

28. 歇步下冲拳

29. 马步双挂拳

30. 跪步双虎爪

31. 虚步冲拳推掌

32. 并步抱拳

收势

Names of the Movements

Preparatory posture

Section 1

1. Thrust fist and push palm in an empty stance

2. Hold fist and palm together in a feet-together stance

3. Side fist thrust in a left bow stance

4. Jieqiao (Cut "bridge") in a left bow stance

5. Quanqiao (Move around the "bridge") and thrust palms forward in a bow stance

6. Lianhuanzhang (Linked palm) in a horse stance

7. Double-finger-pushing in a horse stance

8. Thrust palms forward and sink "bridge" in a horse stance

9. Hold fist and palm together in a feet-together stance

10. Kick with the left heel

11. Push finger on a single foot

12. Gaiquan (Thrust down fist) in a kneeling stance

13. Build "bridge" in a right bow stance

14. Guagaiquan (Fists swing overhead) with the body turning around

15. Step back to grapple

16. Side fist thrust in a right bow stance

Section 2

17. Rein with hands and step down on the ground with the left leg

18. Push palms in a dragon-riding stance

19. Chop "bridge" in a single fold stance

20. Strike out one fist with the other upheld in a right bow stance

21. Throw fist left and right in a bow stance

22. Side fist thrust in a left bow stance

23. Crane's beak in an empty stance

24. Separate palms and do a hook kick

25. Separate feet and hold up palm

26. Push palms in a dragon-riding stance

27. Butterfly palm with the Qilin step and the left bow stance

28. Thrust fist down in a seated stance

29. Shuangguaquan (Two fists swing and strike from overhead) in a horse stance

30. Double tiger claw in a kneeling stance

31. Thrust fist and push palm in an empty stance

32. Hold fist and palm together in a feet-together stance

Closing posture

232

预备势　　　　　　　　　　　　　　　　　　　Preparatory posture

（1）两脚并步，直腿站立；直臂，两掌贴靠于两腿外侧；目视前方。［图6-45（1）］

（2）两腿不动，两掌变拳提抱于腰间，拳心向上；目视前方。［图6-45（2）］

要点：挺膝，夹腿，收腹，敛臀，立腰，提神降气。

(1) Stand with both feet together with straight legs. Place both palms against the outside of the legs, arms straight. Look straight ahead. [Fig. 6-45(1)]

(2) Keep the legs still. Change palms into fists and withdraw them to the waist, the fist centers facing upward. Look straight ahead. [Fig. 6-45(2)]

Key points: Straighten knees. Squeeze legs togeher. Draw in belly, hold back buttocks and keep the waist straight up. Keep spirits up and lower the qi.

图 6-45　预备势（1）　　　　图 6-45　预备势（2）
Fig. 6-45 Preparatory posture (1)　　Fig. 6-45 Preparatory posture (2)

第一段 Section 1

1.虚步冲拳推掌   Thrust fist and push palm in an empty stance

（1）右脚向右前上步，脚尖外展，膝微屈；同时腰微右转，右拳提至右胸前，拳心向下；左拳变掌经上弧形摆至右胸前，掌指向上，掌心与右拳面相对；目视右拳。［图6-46（1）］

（2）左脚向前上半步，脚尖点地成左虚步；同时腰微左转，右拳与左掌向前冲拳、推掌，两臂伸直，与肩同高、同宽，左掌心与右拳面均向前；目视前方。［图6-46（2）］

要点：右脚与左脚上步时重心下沉，虚实分明，冲拳、推掌发力于腰，眼随手动。

(1) Step forward to the right with the right foot, toes turning out and the knee slightly bent. At the same time, turn the waist slightly right, and lift the right fist to the right side of the chest, the fist center facing downward. Change the left fist into a palm and swing it in an arc shape to the right side of the chest, the palm fingers facing upward, and the palm center facing the right fist surface. Look at the right fist. [Fig. 6-46(1)]

(2) Make a half-step forward with the left foot. The tiptoes slightly touch the ground and form a left empty stance. At the same time, turn the waist slightly left, thrust the right fist and push the left palm forward. Straighten both arms at shoulder height and shoulder-width apart. Both the left palm center and the right fist surface face forward. Look straight ahead. [Fig. 6-46(2)]

Key points: When stepping with the right and left foot, lower the center of gravity. Differentiate between "Xu" and "Shi" (Make clear of empty and solid movements). Exert strength from the waist when thrusting the fist and pushing the palm. Eyes follow the movement of hands.

图 6-46　虚步冲拳推掌（1）
Fig. 6-46 Thrust fist and push
palm in an empty stance (1)

图 6-46　虚步冲拳推掌（2）
Fig. 6-46 Thrust fist and push
palm in an empty stance (2)

2. 并步抱拳　　　　　Hold fist and palm together in a feet-together stance

（1）左脚向左后撤步，两膝微屈；同时腰微右转，左掌变拳与右拳回拉至胸前，拳面相对；目视右拳。［图6-47（1）］

（2）右脚向右后撤步，两腿屈膝；同时腰微左转，两臂外旋，两拳经上反臂挂于肩上，拳心向下；目视前方。［图6-47（2）］

（3）左脚向右脚并步，两腿伸直；同时两拳继续挂收至腰间，拳心向上；目视前方。［图6-47（3）］

要点：左、右脚向左、右后撤步，上肢手法清晰、动作干脆，眼随手动。

(1) Step back to the left with the left foot, and bend the knees. At the same time, turn the waist slightly to the right, change the left palm into a fist, pull it back to the front of the chest together with the right fist, with palm surfaces facing each other. Look at the right fist. [Fig. 6-47(1)]

(2) Step back to the right with the right foot, and bend the knees. At the same time, turn the waist slightly to the left, rotate both arms outward, and then hang both fists upside down on shoulders after moving them in an up-front direction, the palm centers facing downward. Look straight ahead. [Fig. 6-47(2)]

(3) Move the left foot to right and form a feet-together stance, both legs straight. At the same time, keep holding both fists on the waist with fist centers facing downward. Look straight ahead. [Fig. 6-47(3)]

Key points: Step back to the left or right with the left or right foot. Make clear-cut movements of upper limbs. Eyes follow the movement of hands.

图 6-47　并步抱拳（1）
Fig. 6-47 Hold fist and palm together in a feet-together stance (1)

图 6-47　并步抱拳（2）
Fig. 6-47 Hold fist and palm together in a feet-together stance (2)

图 6-47　并步抱拳（3）
Fig. 6-47 Hold fist and palm together in a feet-together stance (3)

3. 左弓步侧冲拳　　　　　　　　Side fist thrust in a left bow stance

（1）左脚向左侧开步，两腿屈膝，重心偏于右侧成半马步；同时腰微右转，左拳变掌经体前弧形摆按至右胸前，掌心向右；目视左掌。［图6-48（1）］

(1) Step to the left with the left foot. Bend the knees and put more weight on the right side to form a half horse stance. At the same time, turn the waist slightly right. Chang the left fist into a palm, and swing it in an arc shape to the right side of the chest through the front, the palm facing right. Look at the left palm. [Fig. 6-48(1)]

图 6-48　左弓步侧冲拳（1）
Fig. 6-48 Side fist thrust in a left bow stance (1)

（2）右脚蹬地，右腿内转挺膝伸直成左弓步；同时腰微左转，右拳向右侧冲出，拳眼向上，臂与肩平；左掌变拳收至腰间，拳心向上；目视右拳，同时发声"嗨"。［图6-48（2）］

(2) Form a left bow stance after pushing the right foot against the ground and turning the right leg inward before straightening the knee. At the same time, turn the waist slightly left, and thrust the right fist to the right, the fist eye facing upward and the arm at shoulder height. Change the left palm into a fist and withdraw it to the waist, the fist center facing upward. Look at the right fist, and make an utterance of "hi" at the same time. [Fig. 6-48(2)]

图 6-48　左弓步侧冲拳（2）
Fig. 6-48 Side fist thrusting in a left bow stance (2)

要点：左脚开步时，身体重心先下沉，腰微右转，闭气蓄劲；侧冲拳时注重力起于根。

Key points: Lower the center of gravity first before stepping to the left with the left foot. Hold breath to store up energy when turning the waist right. Exert strength from the root when thrusting fist from the side.

4. 左弓步截桥   Jieqiao (Cut "bridge") in a left bow stance

（1）右腿屈膝并微外展；同时腰微右转，右拳收至腰间，拳眼向上；目视右拳。［图6-49（1）］

（2）右脚蹬地，右腿内转挺膝伸直成左弓步；同时腰微左转，右臂外旋，以前臂尺骨侧（小指侧）为力点向右侧偏左方向截击，拳心斜向上；目视右拳。［图6-49（2）］

要点：右腿的先屈后伸，目的是加大截桥的发力，体现了力起于根的特点，应倍加强调右腿的蹬、扣、转的用力顺序。

(1) Bend the right knee and turn it slightly outward. At the same time. turn the waist slightly right, and withdraw the right fist to the waist, the fist eye facing upward. Look at the right fist. [Fig. 6-49(1)]

(2) Form a left bow stance after pushing the right foot against the ground and straightening the knee. At the same time, turn the waist slightly left, rotate the right arm outward and make a cutting strike to the right side by exerting strength from the ulnar side of the forearm (the little finger side), both fist centers facing obliquely upward. Look at the right fist. [Fig. 6-49(2)]

Key points: The purpose of bending and then extending the right leg is to increase the strength of cutting "bridge", which embodies the characteristics of exerting strength from the root. More emphasis should be placed on the order of strength exertion, i.e., kicking, twisting, and turning.

（正面图）
图 6-49　左弓步截桥（1）
Fig. 6-49 Jieqiao (Cut "bridge") in
a left bow stance (1)

图 6-49　左弓步截桥（2）
Fig. 6-49 Jieqiao (Cut "bridge") in
a left bow stance (2)

5. 弓步圈桥标掌　　　Quanqiao (Move around the "bridge") and thrust palms forward in a bow stance

（1）步不动，右拳变掌，掌心斜向下；目视右掌。［图6-50（1）］

（2）右腿屈膝并微外展；同时腰微右转，右掌向下经右向左前弧形画一圈后收至腰间，掌心向下；目视右掌。［图6-50（2）］

(1) Keep the stance. Change the right fist into a palm, with the palm center facing obliquely upward. Look at the right palm. [Fig. 6-50(1)]

(2) Bend the right knee and turn it slightly outward. At the same time, turn the waist slightly right, draw a circle with the right palm down through the right to left front in an arc shape and then withdraw it to the waist, with the palm facing down. Look at the right palm. [Fig. 6-50(2)]

图 6-50　弓步圈桥标掌（1）
Fig. 6-50 Quanqiao (Move around the "bridge") and thrust palms forward in a bow stance (1)

图 6-50　弓步圈桥标掌（2）
Fig. 6-50 Quanqiao (Move around the "bridge") and thrust palms forward in a bow stance (2)

（3）右腿内转挺膝伸直成左弓步；同时腰微左转，右掌直线向右侧标出，掌心向下，臂与肩平；目视右掌。[图6-50（3）]

(3) Form a left bow stance after turning the right leg inward and straightening the knee. At the same time, turn the waist slightly left, and thrust the right palm straight to the right side with the palm facing downward at shoulder height. Look at the right palm. [Fig. 6-50(3)]

图 6-50　弓步圈桥标掌（3）
Fig. 6-50 Quanqiao (Move around the "bridge") and thrust palms forward in a bow stance (3)

要点：右圈时按逆时针方向运行，以腰带臂，眼随手动；标掌时发力于腿，传于腰，达于指尖，发力快脆。

Key points: When circling with the right palm, move it counterclockwise. Use the waist to drive arms. Eyes follow the movement of hands. When thrusting palms, exert strength from the leg, and convey it through the waist to fingertips. Exert strength in a fast and smooth way.

6. 马步连环掌　　　　　　Lianhuanzhang (Linked palm) in a horse stance

（1）右脚向后稍踏步，两腿屈膝半蹲；同时腰微左转，右掌随前臂外旋屈肘收至左腰侧，左拳变掌置于右掌下，两掌心均向上；目视右掌。〔图6-51（1）〕

（2）身体转正成马步；同时右掌与左掌分别随转腰向正前方的上下攻出，两臂成半圆，右掌与胸同高，左掌与腹同高，掌心均向下，力达小指侧；目视右掌。〔图6-51（2）〕

要点：发力于腰，两臂成圆，收腹、含胸。

(1) Take a small step back with the right foot, and then bend both knees to make a half squat. At the same time, turn the waist slightly left. Draw back the right palm to the left side of the waist while rotating the forearm outward and bending the elbow. Change the left fist into a palm and place it under the right palm, both palms facing upward. Look at the right palm. [Fig. 6-51(1)]

(2) Turn the body to make it face forward and form a horse stance. At the same time, thrust both the right and the left palm straight forward in a up and down direction respectively with the turning of the waist, arms in a semicircle, the right palm at chest height, the left palm at belly height, and both palm centers facing down. Convey the strength to the sides of the little fingers. Look at the right palm. [Fig. 6-51(2)]

Key points: Exert strength from the waist. Make arms in a shape of a circle. Draw in belly and chest.

图 6-51　马步连环掌（1）
Fig. 6-51 Lianhuanzhang (Linked palm) in a horse stance (1)

图 6-51　马步连环掌（2）
Fig. 6-51 Lianhuanzhang (Linked palm) in a horse stance (2)

7. 马步双推指   Double-finger-pushing in a horse stance

（1）马步不动；左掌由下经右臂内侧弧形挑至左肩前，掌指向上，肘下沉；目视左掌。［图6-52（1）］

（2）右掌经外向下沿左臂内侧弧形挑至右肩前，掌指向上，肘下沉，两臂与肩同高、同宽；目视前方。［图6-52（2）］

（3）步仍不动；两掌变单指手，翘指坐腕，手心向前；目视前方。［图6-52（3）］

(1) Stay in a horse stance. Lift the left palm from the bottom through the inner side of the right arm to the front of the left shoulder, the palm fingers facing upward. Lower the elbow. Look at the left palm. [Fig. 6-52(1)]

(2) Lift the right palm from the outside to the inside of the left arm in an arc to the front of the right shoulder, the palm fingers facing upward. Lower the elbow. Keep arms at shoulder height and shoulder-width apart. Look straight ahead. [Fig. 6-52(2)]

(3) Still keep the stance. Change both palms into the single-finger position, lowering the wrists and keeping the two fingers upright. Both palms face forward. Look straight ahead. [Fig. 6-52(3)]

图 6-52　马步双推指（1）　　图 6-52　马步双推指（2）　　图 6-52　马步双推指（3）
Fig. 6-52 Double-finger-pushing in a horse stance (1)　　Fig. 6-52 Double-finger-pushing in a horse stance (2)　　Fig. 6-52 Double-finger-pushing in a horse stance (3)

（4）两臂屈肘，两指挑至肩上，两手心斜向上，两肘正对前方；目视右肘。［图6-52（4）］

（5）两肘下沉，两指收至腰侧，手心斜向前下方；目视左指。［图6-52（5）］

（6）两指用劲慢慢向前推出，臂与肩平，沉肘、坐腕、翘指；目视前方［图6-52（6）］。重复（4）~（6）的动作。

(4) Bend the elbows. Lift the two fingers to the shoulders, both palms facing obliquely upward. Both elbows face forward. Look at the right elbow. [Fig. 6-52(4)]

(5) Sink the elbows, and draw the two fingers back to the waist, with both palms facing obliquely downward. Look at the left finger. [Fig. 6-52(5)]

(6) Exert strength with the two fingers and push them forward slowly. The arms are at shoulder height. Lower the wrists and keep the two fingers upright. Look straight ahead. Repeat the movements of (4), (5), and (6). [Fig. 6-52(6)]

图 6-52　马步双推指（4）
Fig. 6-52 Double-finger-pushing in a horse stance (4)

图 6-52　马步双推指（5）
Fig. 6-52 Double-finger-pushing in a horse stance (5)

图 6-52　马步双推指（6）
Fig. 6-52 Double-finger-pushing in a horse stance (6)

要点：马步沉稳，两臂刚劲有力，手法清晰。

Key points: Keep the horse stance stable. Be strong and forceful with the arms. Make clear-cut movements of the hands.

8. 马步标掌沉桥

Thrust palms forward and sink "bridge" in a horse stance

（1）与马步双推指（4）动作相同。［图6-53（1）］

（2）与马步双推指（5）动作相同。［图6-53（2）］

(1) It is the same with the (4) of double-finger-pushing in a horse stance. [Fig. 6-53(1)]

(2) It is the same with the (5) of double-finger-pushing in a horse stance. [Fig. 6-53(2)]

图6-53 马步标掌沉桥（1）
Fig. 6-53 Thrust palms forward and sink "bridge" in a horse stance (1)

图6-53 马步标掌沉桥（2）
Fig. 6-53 Thrust palms forward and sink "bridge" in a horse stance (2)

（3）马步不动；两指变掌快速向前标出，掌心相对，臂与肩同高、同宽；目视前方。［图6-53（3）］

（4）马步仍不动；两掌以前臂小指侧为力点快速下沉，变掌指向上；目视前方。［图6-53（4）］

(3) Keep the horse stance. Thrust both palms forward quickly, with the palms facing each other, arms at shoulder height and shoulder-width apart. Look straight ahead. [Fig. 6-53(3)]

(4) Still keep the horse stance. Use the sides of both little fingers of forearms as the point of exerting strength, and make arms sink quickly, palms fingers facing upward. Look straight ahead. [Fig. 6-53(4)]

图 6-53　马步标掌沉桥（3）
Fig. 6-53 Thrust palms forward and sink "bridge" in a horse stance (3)

图 6-53　马步标掌沉桥（4）
Fig. 6-53 Thrust palms forward and sink "bridge" in a horse stance (4)

要点：马步沉稳，两臂刚劲有力，手法清晰。

Key points: Keep the horse stance stable. Be strong and forceful with the arms. Make clear-cut movements of the hands.

9. 并步抱拳   Hold fist and palm together in a feet-together stance

（1）步不动，腰微右转；同时两掌变拳随屈肘收至胸前，拳心向下；目视两拳。［图6-54（1）］

（2）两脚微蹬地跳起，成并步；两臂外旋，两拳经上向前反臂挂抱于腰间，拳心向上；目视前方。［图6-54（2）］

要点：两拳先动，当圈绕反臂挂至腹前时，两脚轻轻蹬地跳起；并步与抱拳一致，手、眼、脚步配合完整，动作显示灵巧自如的特点。

(1) Stand still. Turn the waist slightly right while changing both palms into fists and draw them back to the front of the chest, with palm centers facing downward. Look at both fists. [Fig. 6-54(1)]

(2) Jump and land into a feet-together stance after slightly pushing both feet against the ground. Rotate both arms outward, and then hang both fists upside down on the waist after moving them in an up-front direction, the fist centers facing upward. Look straight ahead. [Fig. 6-54(2)]

Key points: Move the fists first. When rotating arms outward and hanging them upside down in front of the belly, slightly push both feet against the ground and jump. Stand with feet together while holding fist and palm together. Hand, eyes and steps should be well coordinated. The movements should be completed skillfully and with ease.

图 6-54　并步抱拳（1）
Fig. 6-54 Hold fist and palm together
in a feet-together stance (1)

图 6-54　并步抱拳（2）
Fig. 6-54 Hold fist and palm together
in a feet-together stance (2)

10. 左蹬脚　　　　　　　　　　　　　　　Kick with the left heel

（1）两腿屈膝，右脚向前上步，脚尖外展，左脚跟离地成拐步；同时腰微右转；目视左侧。［图6-55（1）］

（2）右腿直立支撑，左腿屈膝抬起，以脚跟为力点向前蹬出，高与腰齐，挺膝勾脚；目视前方。［图6-55（2）］

要点：两腿屈膝重心下降时，眼向右环视，右脚上步时目视左侧；蹬脚要由屈到伸，发力快脆。

(1) Bend both knees. Step forward with the right foot, turn toes outward, lift the left heel off the ground, and form a guaibu (cross-legged) stance. At the same time, turn the waist slightly right. Look left. [Fig. 6-55(1)]

(2) Keep the right leg straight for independent support. Bend the left knee and lift it up, exert strength from the heel and kick forward at waist height. Keep the knee straight and turn the toes upward. Look straight ahead. [Fig. 6-55(2)]

Key points: When lowering the center of gravity while bending knees, look around to the right. Look left when stepping forward with the right foot. Make a quick and clear-cut kicking strike when extending the leg from its bending position.

图 6-55　左蹬脚（1）　　　　　　　图 6-55　左蹬脚（2）
Fig. 6-55 Kick with the left heel (1)　　Fig. 6-55 Kick with the left heel (2)

11. 独立步推指   Push finger on a single foot

左腿屈膝，左脚向裆下回收，绷脚；同时左拳变单指手向左腿内侧推出，食指翘起，掌心斜向下；目视左指。（图6-56）

要点：屈腿、推指与眼视要一致。

Bend the left knee, draw the left foot to the crotch side, and stretch the foot. At the same time, change the left fist into the singer-finger position and push it forward to the inner side of the left leg, with the index finger up and the palm center facing obliquely downward. Look at the left finger. (Fig. 6-56)

Key points: Bend the leg, push the finger and look at it at the same time.

图 6-56　独立步推指
Fig. 6-56　Push finger on a single foot

12. 跪步盖拳   Gaiquan (Thrust down fist) in a kneeling stance

（1）左脚向前落步；右拳变双指手直线向前标出，手心向下，臂与肩平；左指变掌按至右臂下方，手指向右；目视右指。［图6-57（1）］

（2）动作不停，左脚用力蹬地，右腿向前上摆起使身体腾空；同时右指变拳直臂经下向后上摆起，左掌直推至体前；目视前方。［图6-57（2）］

（3）左、右脚前后落步，两腿屈膝下蹲成跪步；同时右拳经上向前直臂盖至体前，拳心斜向里；左掌回收至右肩前，手心向右；目视右拳。［图6-57（3）］

要点：动作连贯，身体尽量向前跨跃，跪步时右腿微外展，含胸拔背。

(1) Step forward with the left foot. Change the right fist into the double-finger position and thrust it straight forward, with the palm center facing down and arm at shoulder height. Change the left finger position into a palm and press it down under the right arm, with the finger facing right. Look at the right fingers. [Fig. 6-57(1)]

(2) Keep moving. Push the left foot hard against the ground. Swing the right leg forward and lift the body into the air. At the same time, change from the right-finger position into a fist, keep the arm straight, and swing it up to the back side while pushing the left palm straight to the front of the body. Look straight ahead. [Fig. 6-57(2)]

(3) Step back and forth with the left and right foot respectively. Bend the knees, squat down, and form a kneeling stance. At the same time, thump the right fist from the upper side to the front, the fist center facing obliquely inward. Draw the left palm back to the front the right shoulder, the palm center facing right. Look at the right fist. [Fig. 6-57(3)]

Key points: Complete the movements smoothly and coherently. Leap forward as far as possible. Turn the right leg slightly outward when forming the kneeling stance. Draw in chest. Keep the back straight.

图 6-57　跪步盖拳（1）
Fig. 6-57 Gaiquan
(Thrust down fist)
in a kneeling stance (1)

图 6-57　跪步盖拳（2）
Fig. 6-57 Gaiquan
(Thrust down fist)
in a kneeling stance (2)

图 6-57　跪步盖拳（3）
Fig. 6-57 Gaiquan
(Thrust down fist)
in a kneeling stance (3)

13. 右弓步架桥   Build "bridge" in a right bow stance

（1）右脚向右前上步，脚尖向右，两腿屈膝，重心偏于左腿成半马步；同时腰微左转，右拳变掌与左掌收至左腰侧，右上左下，掌心均向上；目视前方。［图6-58（1）］

（2）左脚蹬地，左腿内转挺膝伸直成右弓步；同时腰微右转，两臂经上分架于头的斜上方，掌心斜向上，臂呈弧形；目视前方。［图6-58（2）］

要点：右脚向右前上步时沉实而稳固，闭气蓄劲；架桥时发力于左腿的蹬转。

(1) Step forward to the right with the right foot, toes facing right. Bend knees, put more weight slightly on the left side and form a half horse stance. At the same time, turn the waist slightly left, change the right fist into a palm and withdraw it together with the left palm to the left side of the waist, the right one on the top and the left one on the bottom. Both palms face upward. Look straight ahead. [Fig. 6-58(1)]

(2) Push the left foot against the ground. Turn the left leg inward and straighten the knee into a right bow stance. At the same time, turn the waist slightly right, place both arms obliquely above the head, with the palm centers facing upward and arms in arc shape. Look straight ahead. [Fig. 6-58(2)]

Key points: Keep the steps solid and stable when stepping forward to the right with the right foot. Hold breadth and store up energy. Exert strength from the pushing and turning of the left leg when building "bridge".

图 6-58　右弓步架桥（1）
Fig. 6-58 Build "bridge" in a right bow stance (1)

（正面图）
图 6-58　右弓步架桥（2）
Fig. 6-58 Build "bridge" in a right bow stance (2)

14. 回身挂盖拳   Guagaiquan (Fists swing overhead) with the body turning around

（1）左腿屈膝，脚尖外撇；同时腰微左转，两掌变拳，两臂由上落至右侧；目视右拳。［图6-59（1）］

（2）右脚向右前移动半步，脚尖内扣，右腿挺膝伸直成左弓步；同时腰左转，左拳随转体经上反臂挂至左后侧，臂伸直，拳心斜向下；右拳经上扣盖至体前，拳心斜向内；目视前方。［图6-59（2）］

要点：右脚移步转体约180°，挂盖时幅度宜大，以腰带臂，发力在腰。

(1) Bend the left knee, toes facing outward. At the same time, turn the waist slightly left and change both palms into fists. Drop arms to the right side from above. Look at the right fist. [Fig. 6-59(1)]

(2) Make a half step forward to the right with the right foot, toes facing inward. Straighten the right leg and form a left bow stance. At the same time, turn the waist slightly left. The left fist follows the turning of the body and then hangs upside down on the left back side, with the arm straight and fist center facing obliquely downward. Thump the right fist from the upper side to the front, with the arm straight and the fist center facing obliquely inward. Look stright ahead. [Fig. 6-59(2)]

Key points: Turn the body for about 180° when stepping with the right foot. Use the waist to drive arms in guagaiquan with a large range of movements. Exert strength from the waist.

图 6-59　回身挂盖拳（1）
Fig. 6-59 Guagaiquan (Fists swing overhead) with the body turning around (1)

图 6-59　回身挂盖拳（2）
Fig. 6-59 Guagaiquan (Fists swing overhead) with the body turning around (2)

15. 退步格打　　　　　　　　　　　　　Step back to grapple

（1）身体重心微向后移，上体稍立起；同时右拳以肘关节为轴由内经上向外挂挑至右肩前，拳心向内，与脸同高；目视右拳。[图6-60（1）]

（2）左脚向右撤步，脚前掌贴地；同时左拳屈肘由后经下向里挂挑至左肩前，拳心向内，与脸同高；右拳收至腰间，拳心向上；目视左拳。[图6-60（2）]

（3）右脚向后撤步，右腿挺膝伸直成左弓步；同时右拳直线向前平冲，拳心向下；左拳收至腰间，拳心向上；目视前方。[图6-60（3）]

要点：撤步时完成右、左拳的挂挑；退右脚时与右冲拳一致，以加大右冲拳的力度。

(1) Move the center of gravity slightly backward. Keep the upper body slightly upright. At the same time, using the elbow joint as the axis, move the right fist in an inward-upward-outward direction and lift it to the front of the right shoulder, the fist center facing inward at face height. Look at the right fist. [Fig. 6-60(1)]

(2) Step back to the right with the left foot, the forefoot on the ground. At the same time, bend the left elbow, lift the left fist to the front of the left shoulder after moving in a backward-downward-inward direction, the fist center facing inward at face height. Withdraw the right fist to the waist with the fist center facing upward. Look at the left fist. [Fig. 6-60(2)]

(3) Step back with the right foot. Straighten the right leg, keep the knee straight and form a left bow stance. At the same time, thrust the right fist straight forward, with the fist center facing downward. Withdraw the left fist to the waist, with the fist center facing upward. Look straight ahead. [Fig. 6-60(3)]

Key points: Lift the right or left fist before stepping backward. Step back with the right leg and thrust the right fist at the same time, so as to intensify the strength of thrusting.

图 6-60　退步格打（1）　图 6-60　退步格打（2）　图 6-60　退步格打（3）
Fig. 6-60 Step back to grapple (1) Fig. 6-60 Step back to grapple (2) Fig. 6-60 Step back to grapple (3)

16. 右弓步侧冲拳　　　　　　　　　Side fist thrust in a right bow stance

左脚尖内扣，左腿内转挺膝伸直成右弓步；同时腰向右转，右拳收回腰间，拳心向上；左拳随转体向左侧平冲，拳眼向上，与肩同高；目视左拳。（图6-61）

要点：左腿内转与左冲拳一致，力起于根（脚）。

Toes of the right foot face inward. Form a right bow stance after turning the left leg inward before straightening the knee. At the same time, turn the waist to the right. Withdraw the right fist to the waist with the fist center facing upward. Thrust the left fist forward to the left side with the turning of the body, the fist eye facing upward at shoulder height. Look at the left fist. (Fig. 6-61)

Key points: Turn the left leg inward and thrust the fist to the left at the same time. Exert strength from the root (foot).

图 6-61　右弓步侧冲拳
Fig. 6-61 Side fist thrust in a right bow stance

第二段 Section 2

17. 勒手左踩腿   Rein with hands and step down on the ground
                                                      with the left leg

（1）两拳变鹰爪，左鹰爪经腰间与右鹰爪一起摆伸至体前下方；目视两爪。［图6-62（1）］

（2）右腿直立支撑；左腿屈膝抬起，脚尖外展，以脚弓内侧为力点向前下方踩出；同时两鹰爪随屈肘拉至左腰侧，右前左后，手心相对；目视左脚。［图6-62（2）］

要点：两鹰爪向体前伸出时速度较缓，踩腿与勒手顺拉要一致，动作脆快，屈伸明显。

(1) Change both fists into eagle claws. Stretch and swing the left claw through the waist together with the right one to the front lower side. Look at both claws. [Fig. 6-62(1)]

(2) Keep the right leg straight for independent support. Bend the left knee and lift it up, toes facing outward. Step forward down by exerting strength from the inner side of the foot arch. At the same time, pull the claws to the left side of the waist with the bending of elbows, with the right claw in the front and the left one in the back, and claw centers facing each other. Look at the left foot. [Fig. 6-62(2)]

Key points: Be slow when stretching forward the eagle claws. Complete stepping of the leg and the reining (pulling) of claws at the same time. Finish the movements in a fast and smooth way. Make the flexion and extension obvious.

图 6-62　勒手左踩腿（1）
Fig. 6-62 Rein with hands and step down on the ground with the left leg (1)

图 6-62　勒手左踩腿（2）
Fig. 6-62 Rein with hands and step down on the ground with the left leg (2)

18. 骑龙步双推掌　　　　　　　Push palms in a dragon-riding stance

左脚向后落步，前脚掌贴地，左膝跪沉成骑龙步；同时两鹰爪变掌向
体前平推，左肘下沉，左掌心向上；右肘弯曲外撑，右掌心向下；目视前
方。（图6-63）

要点： 落步与推掌一致，屈臂发短劲。

Step back with the left foot, the forefoot on the ground. Keel down with the left
knee into a dragon-riding stance. At the same time, change both eagle claws into palms
and push them forward. Lower the left elbow, with the left palm facing upward while
bending the right elbow and holding it outward, with the right palm facing downward.
Look straight ahead. (Fig. 6-63)

Key points: Step back and push palms at the same time. Use short strength when
bending arms.

图 6-63　骑龙步双推掌
Fig. 6-63　Push palms in a dragon-riding stance

19. 单蝶步劈桥　　　　　　　Chop "bridge" in a single fold stance

（1）左腿屈膝略回收（不贴地）；同时右掌变拳，两臂向两侧预
摆；目视右侧。［图6-64（1）］

（2）左腿不停向左斜后跨摆，右脚蹬地并向左斜后方滑步，左腿屈
膝全蹲，右腿屈膝并以小腿内侧贴地成单蝶步；同时右臂外旋，右拳以尺
骨侧为力点经上向体前下劈，拳心向上，屈肘下沉；左掌经外向上、向里

弧形绕摆至右上臂内侧，掌心向右；目视前方。［图6-64（2）］

要点：摆臂跨跳幅度宜大，向左斜后方落步，劈桥时右臂尽量外旋，屈肘下沉。

(1) Bend the left knee and draw it back slightly (off the ground). At the same time, change the right palm into a fist and swing both arms to sides. Look to the right side. [Fig. 6-64(1)]

(2) Swing the left leg to the left back side like a pendulum. Push the right foot against the ground and make a slide step to the left back. To form a single fold stance, do a full squat with the left leg, kneel on the ground with the right leg, and make the inner side of the calf and ankle touch the ground. At the same time, rotate the right arm outward, and chop it down after it moves in an upward-forward direction by exerting strength from the ulnar side, with the fist center facing upward and the bended elbow sinking. Swing the left palm to the inner side of the right upper arm after it moves in an arc shape in an outside-upside-inside direction, with the palm center facing right. Look straight ahead. [Fig. 6-64(2)]

Key points: Swing the arm and the leg with a large range of movements. Step back to the left back side. When chopping "bridge", rotate the right arm outward as much as possible. Lower the elbow and bend it.

图 6-64　单蝶步劈桥（1）　　　　图 6-64　单蝶步劈桥（2）
Fig. 6-64 Chop "bridge" in a single fold stance (1)　Fig. 6-64 Chop "bridge" in a single fold stance (2)

20. 右弓步架打

Strike out one fist with the other upheld in a right bow stance

（1）身体起立，右脚向右前上步，脚尖向右，两腿屈膝成半马步；同时腰微左转，左掌变拳与右拳一起收至左腰侧，右上左下，两拳心均向上；目视右拳。［图6-65（1）］

（2）左脚蹬地，左腿内转挺膝伸直成右弓步；同时右拳上架于头前上方，左拳向前平冲，拳眼向上；目视左拳。［图6-65（2）］

要点：右脚上步，腰微左转；半马步时闭气蓄劲；架打时发力于左脚蹬转。

(1) Stand up and step forward to the right with the right foot, toes facing right. Bend both knees to form a half horse stance. At the same time, turn the waist slightly left, change the left palm into a fist and withdraw it to the waist together with the right fist, with the right fist on the top and the left one on the bottom, and both fist centers facing upward. Look at the right fist. [Fig. 6-65(1)]

(2) Push the left foot against the ground, turn the left leg inward and straighten the knee to form a right bow stance. At the same time, uphold the right fist above the head, and thrust the left fist forward with the fist eye facing upward. Look at the left fist. [Fig. 6-65(2)]

Key points: Step up with the right foot. Turn the waist slightly left. Hold breadth and store up energy when forming the half horse stance. Exert strength from the pushing and turning of the left foot in the striking and upholding of the fists.

图 6-65　右弓步架打（1）
Fig. 6-65 Strike out one fist with the other upheld in a right bow stance (1)

图 6-65　右弓步架打（2）
Fig. 6-65 Strike out one fist with the other upheld in a right bow stance (2)

21. 弓步左右抛拳　　　　Throw fist left and right in a bow stance

（1）左脚向左前上步，屈膝，右腿内转并略向左脚滑动，挺膝伸直成左弓步；同时腰微左转，左臂经下摆至左后侧成平举，拳心向下；右拳随转腰下落直臂向右上方弧形抛起，拳眼向后；目视右前方。［图6-66（1）］

（2）右脚向右前上步，屈膝，左腿内转并略向右脚滑动，挺膝伸直成右弓步；同时腰微右转，右拳直臂下落摆至右后侧成平举，拳心向下；左拳随转腰直臂向左上方弧形抛起，拳眼向后；目视左前方。［图6-66（2）］

要点：左、右脚尽量向横线上步；臂的抢摆幅度宜大，以腰带臂，前踩后蹬对称用力。

(1) Step forward to the left with the left foot, bend the knee, turn the right leg inward and slightly slide to the left foot. Keep the knee straight and form a left bow stance. At the same time, turn the waist slightly left, swing the left arm from the bottom to the left back side, and hold it flat, with the fist center facing downward. Drop the right fist and throw it up to the right in an arc shape with the turning of the body, the fist eye facing backward. Look at the right front side. [Fig. 6-66(1)]

(2) Step forward to the right with the right foot, bend the knee, turn the left leg inward and slightly slide to the right foot. Keep the knee straight and form a right bow stance. At the same time, turn the waist slightly right, swing the right arm from the bottom to the right back side, and hold it flat, with the fist center facing downward. Drop the left fist and throw it up to the left in an arc shape with the turning of the body, the fist eye facing backward. Look at the left front side. [Fig. 6-66(2)]

Key points: Step forward with the left or right foot to the left or right side in a straight line. Swing the arm with a large range of movements, using the waist to drive the arm. Exert symmetrical strength on stepping forward and kicking backward with heel.

图 6-66　弓步左右抛拳（1）
Fig. 6-66 Throw fist left and right in a bow stance (1)

图 6-66　弓步左右抛拳（2）
Fig. 6-66 Throw fist left and right in a bow stance (2)

22. 左弓步侧冲拳　　　　　　　Side fist thrust in a left bow stance

右脚内扣，右腿挺膝伸直成左马步；同时腰向左转，右拳由后经腰间向右侧平冲，拳眼向上；左拳由上收至腰间，拳心向上；目视右拳。（图 6-67）

要点：右脚跟蹬地外转使力由下至上发出，贯于拳面；冲拳时肘微屈下沉，发短劲。

Bend the right foot downward. Straighten the right knee to form a left bow stance while turning the waist to the left. Thrust the right fist to the right through the waist with the fist eye facing upward. Withdraw the left fist from above to the waist, with the fist center facing upward. Look at the right fist. (Fig. 6-67)

Key points: Use the right heel to push against the ground and turn it outward, so that the strength is sent from the bottom to the top and passes through the fist surface. Slightly bend the elbow and lower it when thrusting the fist. Use short strength.

图 6-67　左弓步侧冲拳
Fig. 6-67　Side fist thrust in a left bow stance

23. 虚步鹤嘴手　　　　　　　　　　　Crane's beak in an empty stance

（1）左脚稍向前活步，同时右拳变掌，以腕为轴沿逆时针方向绕一圈后变鹤嘴手，指尖向外；目视右手。右脚向前上半步，脚尖点地成右虚步；同时腰微右转，左拳变鹤嘴手从腰间略向外、向右前方弧形啄击，指尖斜向右；右鹤嘴手随屈肘拉至右胸前，指尖斜向外；目视左手。［图6-68（1）］

（2）右脚踏实，左脚向前上半步，脚尖点地成左虚步；同时腰微左转，右鹤嘴手略经外弧形向左前方啄击，指尖斜向左；左鹤嘴手随屈肘拉至左胸前，指尖斜向外；目视右手。［图6-68（2）］

要点：鹤嘴手啄击时手行弧线，幅度宜小，以腰带臂左右转动；指尖斜向外，意指啄击太阳穴。

(1) Make a small moving step forward with the left foot. At the same time, change the left fist into a palm, use the wrist as the axis, and then change the palm into a crane's beak after moving it around counterclockwise, with fingers facing outside. Look at the right hand. Make a half step forward with the right foot, tiptoes slightly touching the ground and forming a right empty stance. At the same time, turn the waist slightly right, change the left fist into a crane's beak, and make a pecking strike outward from the waist to the right front side, with the fingers facing obliquely right. Pull the right

crane's beak to the right side of the chest with the bending of the elbow, fingertips facing obliquely outward. Look at the left hand. [Fig. 6-68(1)]

(2) Keep the right foot firm on the ground. Make a half step forward with the left foot, tiptoes slightly touching the ground and forming a left empty stance. At the same time, turn the waist slightly left, change the right fist into a crane's beak, and make a pecking strike outward from the waist to the left front side, with the fingers facing obliquely left. Pull the left crane's beak to the left side of the chest with the bending of the elbow, fingertips facing obliquely outward. Look at the right hand. [Fig. 6-68(2)]

Key points: Move the hands with a small range of movements in the pecking strike of cranes' peaks. Use the waist to drive arms to turn left or right, with fingertips facing obliquely outward, meaning pecking at the temple.

图 6-68　虚步鹤嘴手（1）
Fig. 6-68 Crane's beak in an empty stance (1)

图 6-68　虚步鹤嘴手（2）
Fig. 6-68 Crane's beak in an empty stance (2)

24. 分掌弹踢   Separate palms and do a hook kick

（1）左脚向前活步，身体重心向前移动；同时腰向前转正，两鹤嘴手变掌，左掌经外弧形摆至体前与右掌交叠，左掌在前，掌心斜向前；目视两掌。[图6-69（1）]

（2）左腿直立支撑，右腿屈膝抬起后再以脚尖为力点向前弹踢，绷脚挺膝；同时两掌分别向左右侧横摆，掌心均向下，指尖略内扣；目视前方。[图6-69（2）]

要点：分掌、弹踢动作一致，发力快脆，收腹收胯。

(1) Make a moving step forward with the left foot. Move the center of gravity forward. At the same time, turn the waist and make it face forward while changing both cranes' beaks into palms. Swing the left palm in an arc shape through the outside to the front of the body and overlap it with the right palm, with the left one in the front and the palm center facing obliquely forward. Look at both palms. [Fig. 6-69(1)]

(2) Keep the left leg straight for support. After bending the right knee and lifting it up, do a hook kick forward by exerting strength from tiptoes, stretching the foot and keeping the knee straight. At the same time, swing both palms horizontally to the left and right side respectively, with both palms facing downward, and finger tips slightly facing inward. Look straight ahead. [Fig. 6-69(2)]

Key points: Separate palms and do a hook kick at the same time. Exert strength in a fast and smooth way. Draw in belly and hips.

图 6-69　分掌弹踢（1）   图 6-69　分掌弹踢（2）
Fig. 6-69 Separate palms and do a hook kick (1)   Fig. 6-69 Separate palms and do a hook kick (2)

25. 分步撑掌   Separate feet and hold up palm

（1）右脚落地，两膝微屈；同时左掌由左侧经上弧形按至体前，臂内旋，指尖向右；右掌收至腰间，掌心向上；目视左掌。［图6-70（1）］

（2）右脚跟外转，两腿屈膝半蹲成马步；同时腰向左转 90°，右掌随右臂内旋向右侧撑切，力达小指侧，指尖向内，高与腰齐；左掌屈收至右肩内侧，掌心向右；目视右掌。［图6-70（2）］

要点：踏步（右脚落地）按掌沉重有力，马步撑掌发力于腰。

(1) Land the right foot and slightly bend both knees. At the same time, press the left palm to the front of the body after moving it in an arc shape in a left-upward-forward direction, rotating the arm inward and making the fingertips face right. Withdraw the right palm to the waist, the palm center facing upward. Look at the left palm. [Fig. 6-70(1)]

(2) Turn the right heel out, bend both knees and do a half squat to form a horse stance. At the same time, turn the waist left for 90°. Hold the right palm and cut it to the right while rotating the right arm inward. Convey strength to the sides of the little fingers, with fingertips facing inward at waist height. Lower the elbow and draw back the left palm to the inside of the right shoulder, with the palm facing right. Look at the right palm. [Fig. 6-70(2)]

Key points: Be strong and powerful when stepping (landing the right foot) and pressing the palms. Exert strength from the waist when holding up palm in a horse stance.

图 6-70 分步撑掌（1）   图 6-70 分步撑掌（2）
Fig. 6-70 Separate feet and hold up palm (1)   Fig. 6-70 Separate feet and hold up palm (2)

26. 骑龙步双推掌   Push palms in a dragon-riding stance

（1）右脚向右后活步，两腿屈膝半蹲，重心偏于左腿成半马步；同时腰微左转，两掌收于左侧成蝶掌；目视右侧。［图6-71（1）］

（2）左腿内旋并向右脚稍跟进，屈膝跪沉成骑龙步；同时腰微右转，两掌向前平推，左肘下沉，左掌心向上；右掌心向下，右臂呈弧形；目视两掌。［图6-71（2）］

要点：右脚尽量向右侧横向活步，全脚掌贴地，沉实稳重；推掌时借助左腿内旋和转腰的力量，发劲短促。

(1) Make a moving step backward to the right with the right foot. Bend the knees, do a half squat, put more weight on the left leg and form a half horse stance. At the same time, turn the waist slightly left and withdraw both palms to the left side to form the butterfly palm. Look right. [Fig. 6-71(1)]

(2) Turn the left leg inward and step slightly to the right foot, bend the knee and keel down to form a dragon-riding stance. At the same time, turn the waist slightly right and push both palms forward, lowering the left elbow and making the left palm center face upward. The right palm faces downward. The right arm is in an arc shape. Look at both palms. [Fig. 6-71(2)]

Key points: Try to make a horizontal moving step to the right with the right foot. Keep the whole sole on the ground, solid and stable. Make use of the strength exerted from turning the left leg inward and turning the waist when pushing palms. Exert a short strength.

图 6-71　骑龙步双推掌（1）　　　　图 6-71　骑龙步双推掌（2）
Fig. 6-71 Push palms in a dragon-riding stance (1)　Fig. 6-71 Push palms in a dragon-riding stance (2)

27. 麒麟步左弓步蝶掌

Butterfly palm with the Qilin step
and the left bow stance

（1）左脚经右脚前上步，脚尖外展，两腿屈膝交叉成拐步；同时腰微左转，两掌收于左侧成蝶掌；目视左侧。[图6-72（1）]

（2）右脚由后弧形向左前方上步，脚尖外展，两腿屈膝交叉成拐步；同时腰微右转，两掌由左经上弧形盘绕至右侧成蝶掌；目视右侧。[图6-72（2）]

(1) Step forward with left foot through the front of the right foot, toes turning outward. Bend both knees and cross them to form guaibu (Qilin step). At the same time, turn the waist slightly left, and withdraw both palms to the left side to form the butterfly palm. Look left. [Fig. 6-72(1)]

(2) Step forward to the left with the right foot moving in an arc shape from behind, toes turning outward. Bend both knees and cross them to form guaibu (Qilin step). At the same time, turn the waist slightly right, and move both palms from the left in an arc shape through the upper side to the right side to form the butterfly palm. Look right. [Fig. 6-72(2)]

图 6-72　麒麟步左弓步蝶掌（1）
Fig. 6-72 Butterfly palm with
the Qilin step and the left
bow stance (1)

图 6-72　麒麟步左弓步蝶掌（2）
Fig. 6-72 Butterfly palm with
the Qilin step and the left
bow stance (2)

（3）左脚向左侧上步，脚尖向左，两腿屈膝半蹲，重心偏于右侧成半马步；目视左侧。[图6-72（3）]

（4）右脚蹬地，右腿内转伸直成左弓步；同时腰微左转，两掌左上右下向前推出，两掌心向前，左掌指向上，右掌指向下，两掌根相距10～20厘米；目视两掌。[图6-72（4）]

(3) Step to the left with the left foot, toes facing left. Bend both knees, do a half squat, put more weight on the right side and form a half horse stance. Look left. [Fig. 6-72(3)]

(4) Push the right foot against the ground and turn the leg inward. Straighten the right leg and form a left bow stance. At the same time, turn the waist slightly left, and push both palms forward to the left upper side and right lower side respectively, with both palms facing forward, the left palm fingers facing up, and the right ones facing down. Keep the distance between the two palm roots 10-20 cm. Look at both palms. [Fig. 6-72(4)]

图 6-72　麒麟步左弓步蝶掌（3）
Fig. 6-72 Butterfly palm with the Qilin step and the left bow stance (3)

图 6-72　麒麟步左弓步蝶掌（4）
Fig. 6-72 Butterfly palm with the Qilin step and the left bow stance (4)

要点：左右上步为麒麟步，两腿交叉，一脚脚尖外展，另一脚脚跟离地，重心下沉平稳；两掌以肘关节为轴盘绕，幅度宜小，推掌时发力于腿。

Key points: From the Qilin step by stepping with either the left or the right foot. Cross the legs. Toes of one foot turn outward. Keep the heel of the other foot off ground. Lower the center of gravity and be steady. Move the palms in an arc shape by using the elbow as the axis with a small range of movements. Exert strength from the legs when pushing palms.

28. 歇步下冲拳 Thrust fist down in a seated stance

（1）右脚上步；右掌以腕为轴沿顺时针方向刁缠一圈后变拳，拳心斜向上；左掌变拳收至腰间，拳心向上；目视右拳。［图6-73（1）］

（2）右脚向前上步，脚尖外展，两膝全蹲成歇步；同时左拳向前下冲出，拳心向下；右拳收至腰间，拳心向上；目视左拳。［图6-73（2）］

要点：右脚尽量外展，两腿前后夹紧，上体略前倾。

(1) Step forward with the right foot. Move the right palm around the wrist as the axis in a clockwise direction, and then make the fist center face obliquely upward. Change the left palm into a fist and withdraw it to the waist, the fist center facing upward. Look at the right fist. [Fig. 6-73(1)]

(2) Step up forward with the right foot, toes turning outward. Bend knees, do a full squat and form a seated stance. At the same time, thrust the left fist forward to the downside with the fist center facing downward. Draw back the right fist to the waist, the fist center facing upward. Look at the left fist. [Fig. 6-73(2)]

Key points: Extend the right foot as far as possible. Clamp the legs tightly. The upper body slightly leans forward.

图 6-73　歇步下冲拳（1）
Fig. 6-73 Thrust fist down in a seated stance (1)

图 6-73　歇步下冲拳（2）
Fig. 6-73 Thrust fist down in a seated stance (2)

29. 马步双挂拳   Shuangguaquan (Two fists swing and strike from overhead) in a horse stance

身体起立，腰身右转，右拳伸至腹前，拳心向下；左前臂摆至与右前臂交叉，左拳心向下；目视右侧。左脚向左侧上步，脚尖内扣，两腿屈膝半蹲成马步；同时两拳交叉后经上向两侧分挂，微屈肘下沉，两拳心斜向上；目视左拳。（图6-74）

要点：身体起立并向右转约 90°，眼视右侧；马步挂拳时目视左拳，注意手、眼、步的配合。

Keep the body up and turn the waist to the right. Stretch the right fist to the front of the abdomen, the fist center facing downward. Swing the left fist up and cross it over to the right forearm, the left fist center facing down. Look right. Step to the left with the left foot, toes facing inward. Bend both knees, do a half squat and form a horse stance. At the same time, strike with both fists to both sides after crossing them overhead. Slightly bend the elbows and lower them down, both fist centers facing obliquely upward. Look at the left fist. (Fig. 6-74)

Key points: Stand up and turn to the right side for about 90°. Look right. When the two fists swing and strike from overhead, look at the left fist. Pay attention to the coordination of hands, eyes, and steps.

图 6-74 马步双挂拳

Fig. 6-74 Shuangguaquan (Two fists swing and strike from overhead) in a horse stance

30. 跪步双虎爪　　　　　　　　Double tiger claw in a kneeling stance

（1）身体稍起立，重心偏于左腿；同时两拳变虎爪，两臂内旋下摆至左胯侧，手心向下；目视前下方。［图6-75（1）］

（2）左腿支撑，右腿屈膝抬起；同时腰微右转，两虎爪继续由下经上摆起；目视前方。［图6-75（2）］

(1) Keep the body slightly up. Put more weight on the left leg. At the same time, change both fists into tiger claws, rotate both arms inward and place them to the side of the left hip, the claw centers facing downward. Look forward to the downside. [Fig. 6-75(1)]

(2) Use the left leg for support, bend the right knee and lift it up. At the same time, turn the waist slightly right and swing both tiger claws up from below. Look straight ahead. [Fig. 6-75(2)]

图 6-75　跪步双虎爪（1）
Fig. 6-75 Double tiger claw in a kneeling stance (1)

图 6-75　跪步双虎爪（2）
Fig. 6-75 Double tiger claw in a kneeling stance (2)

（3）左脚蹬地跳起，提膝，右脚落地支撑；同时腰向右转约180°，两虎爪继续由上下摆至右胯侧，手心斜向下；目视右爪。［图6-75（3）］

（4）左脚向前上一大步，右脚随之跟进，两腿屈膝全蹲成跪步；同

时腰微左转，两虎爪向前平推，臂与肩平，略宽于肩，两手心向前；目视前方，同时发声"嗨"。［图6-75（4）］

(3) Push the left foot against the ground, jump and lift the knee. Land the right foot for support while turning the waist to the right for about 180°. Then swing both tiger claws down and place them on the side of the right hip, with both claw centers facing obliquely downward. Look at the right claw. [Fig. 6-75(3)]

(4) Make a big step forward with the left foot, and the right foot follows. Bend both knees and do a full squat to form a kneeling stance. At the same time, turn the waist slightly left, and push both tiger claws straight forward, with arms at shoulder height and a little wider than shoulder width. Both claw centers face forward. Look straight ahead and make an utterance of "hi" at the same time. [Fig. 6-75(4)]

图 6-75　跪步双虎爪（3）　　　图 6-75　跪步双虎爪（4）
Fig. 6-75 Double tiger claw in a kneeling stance (3)　Fig. 6-75 Double tiger claw in a kneeling stance (4)

要点：几个分解动作要连贯，左脚尽量向前跨大步，右脚跟进，跪步时含胸拔背，两臂用力，坐腕翘指。

Key points: For the segments of the movement, be coherent and smooth. Try to make a stride (big step) forward with the left foot, and the right foot fo lows. Draw in chest and keep the back straight in the kneeling stance. Exert strength with both arms. Lower the wrists and keep the fingers upright.

31. 虚步冲拳推掌   Thrust fist and push palm in an empty stance

（1）右脚向前上一大步，脚尖向右，膝微屈；同时腰微右转，右虎爪变拳收至腰间，拳心向上；左虎爪变掌经上弧形摆按至右胸前，掌心向右，掌指向上；目视左掌。［图6-76（1）］

（2）左脚向左前上步，脚尖点地成左虚步；同时腰微左转，右拳、左掌随转体向正前方冲拳、推掌，两臂与肩同高、同宽，右拳心向下，左掌指向上；目视前方。［图6-76（2）］

要点：虚实分明，手法干脆。

(1) Make a big step forward with the right foot, toes facing right and the knee slightly bent. At the same time, turn the waist slightly right, change the right tiger claw into a fist and draw it back to the waist, the fist center facing upward. Change the left tiger claw into a palm and swing it in an arc shape to the right side of the chest, the palm facing right, and the palm fingers facing upward. Look at the left palm. [Fig. 6-76(1)]

(2) Step forward to the left with the left foot. The tiptoes slightly touch the ground and form a left empty stance. At the same time, turn the waist slightly left, thrust the right fist and push the left palm forward with the turning of the body, with arms at shoulder height and shoulder-width apart. The right fist center faces down, and the left palm fingers face up. Look straight ahead. [Fig. 6-76(2)]

Key points: Differentiate between "Xu" and "Shi" (Make clear of empty and solid movements). Make clear-cut and smooth movements of the hands.

图 6-76　虚步冲拳推掌（1）
Fig. 6-76 Thrust fist and push
palm in an empty stance (1)

图 6-76　虚步冲拳推掌（2）
Fig. 6-76 Thrust fist and push
palm in an empty stance (2)

32. 并步抱拳　　　　　　Hold fist and palm together in a feet-together stance

（1）左脚向左后撤步；同时腰微右转，左掌变拳与右拳一起摆至右胸前，拳面相对；目视两拳。［图6-77（1）］

（2）右脚向右侧开步，两膝微屈；同时腰微左转，两臂外旋，两拳摆至肩上，两拳心向下；目视前方。［图6-77（2）］

（3）左脚向右脚并拢直立；同时两拳收抱于腰间，拳心向上；目视正前方。［图6-77（3）］

要点：两脚向左右开步，眼随手动，并步时夹腿、紧臀、收腹，提神降气。

(1) Step back to the left with the left foot. At the same time, turn the waist slightly right, change the left palm into a fist and pull it back to the right side of the chest together with the right fist, with fist surfaces facing each other. Look at both fists. [Fig. 6-77(1)]

(2) Step to the right with the right foot, and bend the knees. At the same time, turn the waist slightly left, rotate both arms outward, and then swing both fists to shoulders, both fist centers facing downward. Look straight ahead. [Fig. 6-77(2)]

(3) Move the left foot to right and form a feet-together stance. At the same time, hold both fists on the waist with fist centers facing upward. Look straight ahead. [Fig. 6-77(3)]

Key points: Step to the left or right with the left or right foot. Eyes follow the movements of hands. In the feet-together stance, clamp legs, hold back buttocks, draw in belly, keep spirits up and lower the qi.

图 6-77　并步抱拳（1）
Fig. 6-77 Hold fist and palm together in a feet-together stance (1)

图 6-77　并步抱拳（2）
Fig. 6-77 Hold fist and palm together in a feet-together stance (2)

图 6-77　并步抱拳（3）
Fig. 6-77 Hold fist and palm together in a feet-together stance (3)

收势   Closing posture

两拳变掌垂于体侧，目视前方。（图6-78）

Change both fists into palms and place them on body sides. Look straight ahead.
(Fig. 6-78)

图 6-78　收势
Fig. 6-78 Closing posture